★

I HEAR AMERICA SINGING!

Folk Songs for American Families

★

I HEAR AMERICA SINGING!
Folk Songs for American Families

Collected and Arranged by Kathleen Krull

Illustrated by Allen Garns

Introductory Note by Arlo Guthrie

Alfred A. Knopf  New York

I am indebted to the solid collection of music books and recordings at the San Diego Public Library; to the Athenaeum Music and Arts Library of La Jolla; to mail-order companies such as Elderly Instruments in Lansing, Michigan; to Garrison Keillor and Minnesota Public Radio's *A Prairie Home Companion* and other radio shows on KPBS (San Diego), KPFK (Los Angeles), and KCRW (Santa Monica); and to my editor, Anne Schwartz, for her consistent vision and constant enthusiasm.

CD arranged and produced by Julian Harris. For a list of performers and details of CD recording, see last page of book.

THIS IS A BORZOI BOOK PUBLISHED BY ALFRED A. KNOPF

Text copyright © 1992 by Kathleen Krull
Illustrations copyright © 1992 by Allen Garns
Music ℗ 2003 by Random House, Inc.

www.randomhouse.com/kids

Library of Congress Control Number: 89-49562
ISBN 0-375-82527-4 (trade with CD) — ISBN 0-375-92527-9 (lib. bdg. without CD)

Manufactured in the United States of America
May 2003
Music engraved by Susan Krul/Multi-Art Music Corporation
10 9 8 7 6 5 4 3 2 1

Copyright acknowledgments appear on p. 146.

To Paul

—K. K.

To Ali, Paul, and Ben

—A. G.

An Introductory Note

by ARLO GUTHRIE

I'm out here somewhere on the road tonight thinking about songs I used to hear and sing when I was a little guy. Last night there was a big full moon up in the sky, and as I stood there in its silvery blue light I remembered a little song my mother used to sing to us kids whenever the moon was full. The past became mixed up with the present. Then there was no past, there was only forever. And I sat there listening to my mother sing once more.

The moon song was one of my mother's favorites, and if we could get her to sing just one song, it wouldn't be too hard for us to get her to sing just one more, and then another, and then we'd be staying up late and soon we'd all fall off to sleep with strange songs and stories in our heads. That was over thirty years ago, but I remember them more clearly now than the mornings after we heard them then.

As you enjoy these songs with others, forget everything else. Let your hearts pour into each other. The moments we spend together are not limited to time or space. They are literally forever with us. Make sure your moments are worthy of eternity.

All the best . . .

Author's Note

Everybody is hereby invited to sing their heads off with this collection of over sixty traditional and contemporary American folk songs!

Since even scholars disagree on an exact definition, maybe the best, truest way to describe folk music is simply as "good songs that have stayed good songs." Some are centuries old but still evoke universal feelings. They speak of ideals, changing the world, good times, hard times, love, community, and the triumph of good over evil. Folk songs teach us about past generations and other places; they can also be full of stress-relieving nonsense. You don't have to go to a concert hall to hear them performed or take years of music lessons to play them. "Folk music creates its own audience," Bob Dylan has said, "because you can take a guitar anywhere, anytime."

These songs were winnowed from a list of literally thousands of possibilities. I've aimed the collection at children ages seven and up, who are discovering the world outside of themselves. Left out were songs I felt were too adult or babyish, mystifying or boring, morbid or cruel, racist or sexist.

In making the final selections, I've tried to strike a regional balance to illustrate the broad canvas of America itself. There's representation "from California to the New York Island" and most states in between, plus a reasonable mix of themes, types, emotions, topics, and historical periods.

Of course, I also chose the songs I liked best. So this book has a number of train songs, for instance, and there's a slight tilt toward the South. And in addition to the durable old favorites, there are several songs making a relatively unusual appearance in a children's book.

To further stimulate a fresh and different feeling, I've organized the material alphabetically. I hope the crazy juxtapositions — "Take Me Out to the Ball Game" next to "Sweet Betsy from Pike," "This Land Is Your Land" next to "There's a Hole in the Bucket," "The Motorcycle Song" next to "The Mockingbird Song" — will make each song stand out and call attention to one another.

Finally, I've kept the piano and guitar arrangements as simple and familiar-sounding as possible without being boring. I've picked keys that are easiest for the average person to sing and play in.

This book was conceived because there was a real need for it. Remembering *The Fireside Book of Folk Songs,* edited by Margaret Boni and illustrated by Alice and Martin Provensen back in 1947, I wanted to help ensure that quality traditional music remain important in the lives of children. The further I pursued this idea—especially when writing the musical arrangements—the more exciting the book became to me as a way of recapturing my past. I hope the same will hold true for the parents of those who use this collection.

I must admit, I sang my head off while working on the book. Now it's your turn. Please feel free to improvise, create your own harmonies, invent your own verses—and bring your own voice to these wonderful songs.

—KATHLEEN KRULL
San Diego

Contents

★

I HEAR AMERICA SINGING!

Folk Songs for American Families

★

ACRES OF CLAMS

CALIFORNIA / PUGET SOUND, WASHINGTON

California gold prospectors sang this song as they headed north, dreaming of being as happy as clams—surrounded *by* clams. The tune derives from an old Irish melody, and the lyrics were said to be written by Judge Francis D. Henry in 1849. By 1889, the year Washington became a state, this was its official song. It's been used as a theme song (with different words) in at least four presidential campaigns. And the last time Pete Seeger heard Woody Guthrie sing, in 1952, he and Guthrie made up verses all night to "Acres of Clams."

Energetically

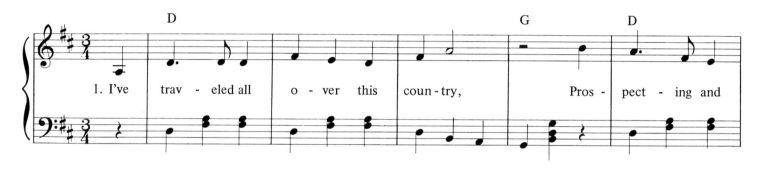

1. I've trav - eled all o - ver this coun - try, Pros - pect - ing and

dig - ging for gold; I've tun - neled, hy - drau - licked, and cra - dled,

And I have been fre - quent - ly sold. And

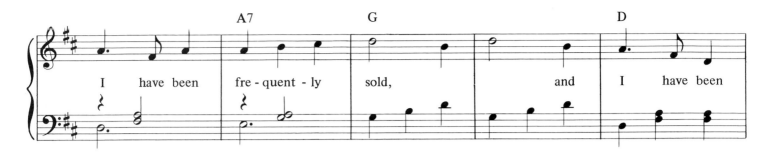

I have been | fre-quent-ly | sold, | and | I have been

fre-quent-ly | sold. | I've | tun-neled, hy - | drau-licked, and

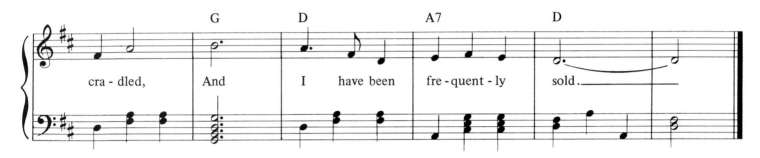

cra - dled, | And | I | have been | fre-quent-ly | sold. _____

2. For one who got wealthy by mining,
   I saw many hundreds get poor.
   I made up my mind to try digging
   For something a little more sure.
       For something a little more sure, etc.

3. I rolled up my grub in a blanket.
   I left all my tools on the ground.
   I started one morning to shank it
   For the country they call Puget Sound.
       For the country they call Puget Sound, etc.

4. And now that I'm used to the climate,
   I think that if man ever found
   A place to live easy and happy,
   That Eden is on Puget Sound.
       That Eden is on Puget Sound, etc.

5. No longer a slave of ambition,
   I laugh at the world and its shams,
   And think of my happy condition,
   Surrounded by acres of clams.
       Surrounded by acres of clams, etc.

ARKANSAS TRAVELER

When Arkansas became a state, in 1836, this "popular air" was its official song. By the 1850s the song was inspiring famous paintings and even a humorous folk drama. Packed houses were charmed by nonsense arguments between a backwoods, philosophical old man and a well-groomed practical traveler, each of whom could play half of this lively fiddler's reel but not the other half.

Zippy

1. Oh, once up-on a time in Ar-kan-sas, An old man sat in his lit-tle cab-in door, And he

fid-dled at a tune that he liked to hear, A jol-ly old_ tune that he played_ by ear. It was

rain - ing_ hard, but the fid-dler did-n't care; He sawed a - way at the pop-u-lar air, Though his

roof tree_ leaked like a wa - ter - fall, That did-n't seem to both - er the man_ at all.

2. A traveler was riding by that day
   And stopped to hear him a-fiddlin' away;
   The cabin was afloat and his feet were wet,
   But still the old man didn't seem to fret.
   So the stranger said, "Now, the way it seems to me,
   You'd better mend your roof," said he.
   But the old man said as he played away:
   "I couldn't mend it now—it's a rainy day."

3. The traveler replied, "That's all quite true,
   But this, I think, is the thing for you to do;
   Get busy on a day that is fair and bright,
   Then patch the old roof till it's good and tight."
   But the old man kept on a-playing at his reel,
   And tapped the ground with his leathery heel.
   "Get along," said he, "for you give me a pain—
   My cabin never leaks when it doesn't rain!"

BARNYARD SONG
◖ or, I Had a Cat

APPALACHIA

Every language has its own animal-noise songs that can erupt into silliness with each addition. This one was a popular play-party song throughout the Southern mountain region. It probably descends from a European song, and it has other American cousins: "I Had a Little Rooster," "Bought Me a Cat" (from Arkansas), and "Old MacDonald Had a Farm."

Okay to act like an animal

* **Repeat these two measures twice in verse three,
three times in verse four, and so on.**

2. I had a dog and the dog pleased me.
   Fed my dog under yonder tree.
   Dog went, "Bowwow,"
   Cat went, "Fiddle-i-fee, fiddle-i-fee."

3. I had a hen and the hen pleased me.
   Fed my hen under yonder tree.
   Hen went, "Ka-ka,"
   Dog went, "Bowwow,"
   Cat went, "Fiddle-i-fee, fiddle-i-fee."

6

4. I had a duck and the duck pleased me.
   Fed my duck under yonder tree.
   Duck went, "Quack, quack,"
   Hen went, "Ka-ka,"
   Dog went, "Bowwow,"
   Cat went, "Fiddle-i-fee, fiddle-i-fee."

5. I had a goose and the goose pleased me.
   Fed my goose under yonder tree.
   Goose went, "Swishy, swashy,"
   Duck went, "Quack, quack," etc.

6. I had a sheep and the sheep pleased me.
   Fed my sheep under yonder tree.
   Sheep went, "Baa, baa,"
   Goose went, "Swishy, swashy," etc.

7. I had a cow and the cow pleased me.
   Fed my cow under yonder tree.
   Cow went, "Moo, moo,"
   Sheep went, "Baa, baa," etc.

8. I had a horse and the horse pleased me.
   Fed my horse under yonder tree.
   Horse went, "Neigh, neigh,"
   Cow went, "Moo, moo," etc.

BEANS IN MY EARS

Words and music: LEN H. CHANDLER

Len Chandler, a contemporary songwriter, claims he wrote this silly song in five minutes, inspired by a Carl Sandburg poem and some old jokes. After a few weeks on the radio, his song was banned (or "black-beaned"), because the Board of Health felt it set a bad example. . . .

Rebellious

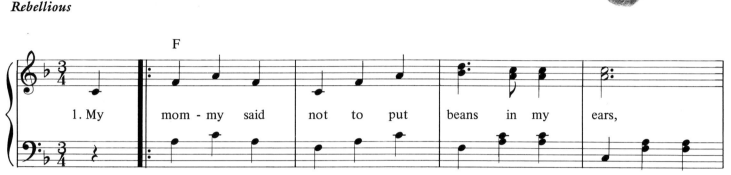

1. My mom-my said not to put beans in my ears,

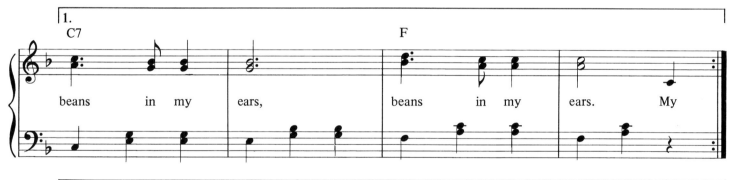

beans in my ears, beans in my ears. My

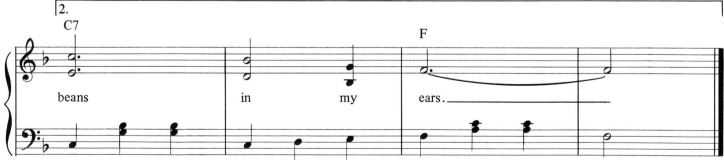

beans in my ears._____

2. Now, why would I want to put beans in my ears,
   Beans in my ears, beans in my ears?
   Oh, why would I want to put beans in my ears,
             beans in my ears?

3. You can't hear your teachers with beans in your ears, etc.

4. Oh, maybe it's fun to have beans in your ears, etc.

5. Hey, Charlie, let's go and put beans in our ears, etc.

6. *What's that you say?* Let's put beans in our ears, etc.

7. *You'll have to speak up!* I've got beans in my ears, etc.

8. Hey, Mommy, I've gone and put beans in my ears, etc.

9. That's nice, son, just don't put those beans
             in your ears, etc.

10. I think that all grownups have beans in their ears, etc.

BUFFALO GALS

BUFFALO, NEW YORK

Cool White, a minstrel singer, wrote this dance tune in 1844—and it's not about female buffaloes! It's about the women of Buffalo, Pittsburgh, Charleston—or wherever Cool White's group happened to be playing. "Buffalo" stuck, after a celebrated version was sung in that town in 1848. Mark Twain used the song in *Tom Sawyer;* it's played at dances in Laura Ingalls Wilder's "Little House" books; and it's still popular today, even used as part of a television-show theme song.

Flirtatiously

1. Buf-fa-lo gals, won't you come out to-night, come out to-night, come out to-night? Buf-fa-lo gals, won't you come out to-night And

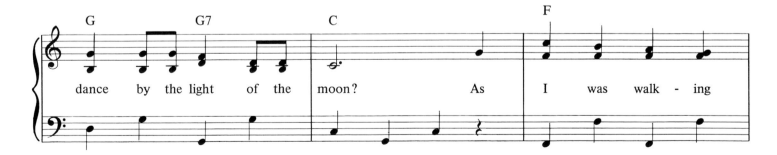

dance by the light of the moon? As I was walk-ing

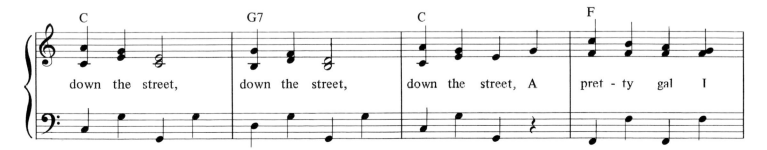

down the street, down the street, down the street, A pret-ty gal I

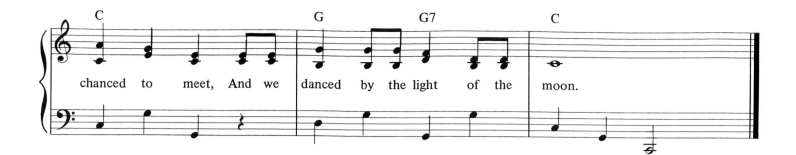

chanced to meet, And we danced by the light of the moon.

2. Oh, yes, pretty boys, we're coming out tonight,
   Coming out tonight, coming out tonight.
   Oh, yes, pretty boys, we're coming out tonight,
   To dance by the light of the moon.

3. I danced with a gal with a hole in her stocking,
   And her heel kept a-rockin' and her toe kept a-knockin'.
   I danced with a gal with a hole in her stocking,
   And we danced by the light of the moon.

CASEY JONES

John Luther Jones, who got his nickname from his hometown of Cayce, Kentucky, was a real person, a well-known train engineer. Substituting for a sick friend one night in 1900, he took the Illinois Central's *Cannonball* out and, near Vaughan, Mississippi, crashed spectacularly into another train. Casey Jones was dead at age twenty-six. Railroading constantly threatened death and disaster, and songs were one way to glamorize workers so crucial to America's expansion. One of forty-five related ballads, this 1909 version of Casey's tragedy is by two railroad men, T. Lawrence Seibert and Eddie Newton.

Pulsing

2. Casey pulled up that Reno hill;
   He whistled for the crossing with an awful shrill.
   The switchman knew by the engine's moan
   That the man at the throttle was Casey Jones.
   He looked at his water and his water was low;
   He looked at his watch and his watch was slow;
   He turned to his fireman and this is what he said:
   "Jim, we're going to reach Frisco, but we'll all be dead."
   Casey Jones—going to reach Frisco,
   Casey Jones—but we'll all be dead, etc.

3. Put in your water and shovel your coal;
   Stick your head out the window, watch those drivers roll;
   I'll drive her till she leaves the rail,
   'Cause I'm eight hours late with the western mail.
   When he was within six miles of the place,
   The number four stared him straight in the face.
   He turned to his fireman, said, "Jim, you better jump,
   'Cause there's two locomotives that are going to bump."
   Casey Jones—two locomotives,
   Casey Jones—going to bump, etc.

4. Casey said, just before he died,
   "There's two more roads that I'd like to ride."
   The fireman said, "Which ones can they be?"
   "The Northern Pacific and the Santa Fe."
   Mrs. Jones sat on her bed a-sighing,
   Just to hear the news that her Casey was dying.
   "Go to bed, children, and hush your crying,
   'Cause you've got another papa on the Salt Lake line."
   Casey Jones—got another papa,
   Casey Jones—on the Salt Lake line, etc.

THE CAT CAME BACK

CHICAGO

This slapstick song is for cat lovers — and also for cat haters. Outrageous fates befall this furry creature, but like a superhero, he just can't be squelched. Harry S. Miller, a Chicago songwriter, wrote this in 1893, using ideas from some old French verses. More verses have been added since, with fates ever more contemporary and "cat" — astrophic. Perhaps you can think up one more verse to use up the cat's ninth life.

Slyly

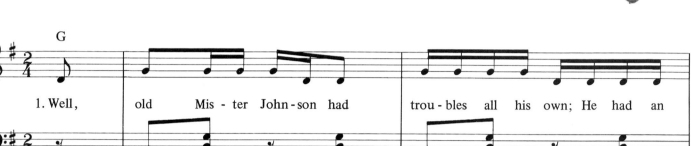

1. Well, old Mis-ter John-son had trou-bles all his own; He had an

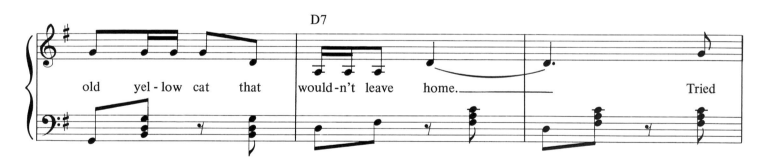

old yel-low cat that would-n't leave home.___ Tried

ev-'ry-thing he knew to get the cat to stay a-way, e-ven took him up to Ca-na-da and

CHORUS

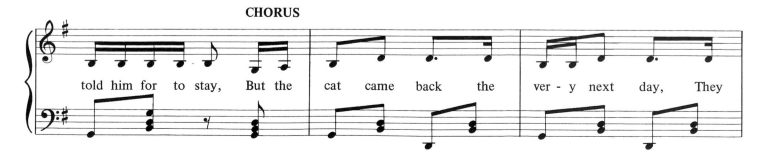

told him for to stay, But the cat came back the ver-y next day, They

14

thought he was a gon-er but the cat came back 'cause he would-n't stay a-way.

2. Well, they gave a boy a dollar for to set the cat afloat,
   And he took him up the river in a sack in a boat;
   Now the fishing it was fine till the news got around
   That the boat was missing and the boy was drowned.
   CHORUS

3. Well, the farmer on the corner said he'd shoot him on sight,
   And he loaded up his gun full of rocks and dynamite.
   The gun went off, heard all over town;
   Little pieces of the man was all that they found.
   CHORUS

4. Now, they gave him to a man going up in a balloon,
   And they told him for to leave him with the man in the moon.
   The balloon it busted, back to earth did head;
   Seven miles away they picked the man up dead.
   CHORUS

5. Well, they finally found a way this cat for to fix;
   They put him in an orange crate on Route 66.
   Come a ten-ton truck with a twenty-ton load,
   Scattered pieces of the orange crate all down the road.
   CHORUS

6. Well, they took him to the shop where the meat was ground,
   And they dropped him in the hopper when the butcher wasn't round.
   Well, the cat disappeared with a bloodcurdling shriek,
   And the town's meat tasted furry for a week.
   CHORUS

7. Then they took him to Cape Canaveral and they put him in a place;
   Shot him in a U.S. rocket going way out in space.
   And they finally thought the cat was out of human reach;
   Next day they got a call from Miami Beach.
   CHORUS

8. The atom bomb fell just the other day;
   The H-bomb fell in the very same way.
   Russia went, England went, and then the U.S.A.;
   The human race was finished without a chance to pray.
   CHORUS

15

CITY OF NEW ORLEANS

Words and music: STEVE GOODMAN

For some reason trains inspire American songs. This contemporary train song was written by Chicagoan Steve Goodman (1948–1984) while he was riding on the train, campaigning for Democrat Edmund Muskie for President. It was popularized by Arlo Guthrie in 1972. The *City of New Orleans* was the real name of an Illinois Central train that ran along the very same route Casey Jones used to travel. Trains today may have the "disappearing railroad blues," but *songs* about trains have become almost more popular than the real thing.

Soothingly

1. Rid-ing on the *Cit-y* of *New* *Or-leans,*

Il-li-nois Cen-tral Mon-day morn-ing rail.

16

Fif - teen cars and fif - teen rest - less rid - ers,_____ three con-

duc - tors and twen-ty -five sacks of mail._____ All a-

long the south - bound od - ys - sey,__ the train pulls out of Kan - ka - kee__ and

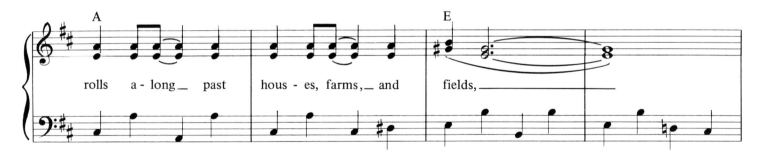

rolls a - long__ past hous - es, farms,__ and fields,_____

Pass - ing towns__ that have no name__ and freight-yards full of old black men,__ and the

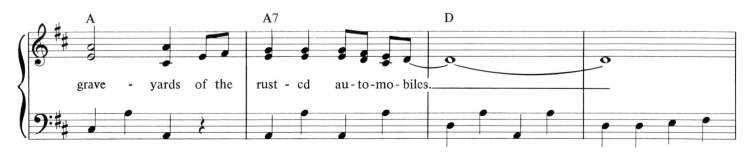

grave - yards of the rust - ed au-to-mo-biles._____

CHORUS

Good morn - ing, A - mer - i - ca, how are you? _____ Said,

don't you know__ me, I'm your na - tive son. I'm the

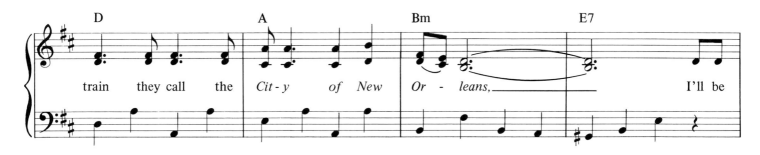

train they call the *Cit - y of New Or - leans,_____ _____ I'll be

gone five hun - dred miles_____ when the day__ is done. _____

2. Dealing card games with the old men in the club car,
   Penny a point, ain't no one keeping score.
   Pass the paper bag that holds the bottle;
   Feel the wheels grumbling 'neath the floor.
   And the sons of Pullman porters, and the sons of engineers,
   Ride their father's magic carpet made of steel.
   Mothers with their babes asleep are rocking to the gentle beat
   And the rhythm of the rails is all they feel.

   CHORUS

3. Nighttime on the *City of New Orleans,*
   Changing cars in Memphis, Tennessee;
   Halfway home, we'll be there by morning,
   Through the Mississippi darkness rolling down to the sea.
   But all the towns and people seem to fade into a bad dream,
   And the steel rail still ain't heard the news.
   The conductor sings his songs again,
   The passengers will please refrain—
   This train's got the disappearing railroad blues.

   CHORUS: Good night, America, how are you, etc.

18

CLEMENTINE

Women were scarce in the California gold-mining camps, so you'd think songs about women would be pleasant and romantic. Not so with unfortunate Clementine. The words and music to this durable ballad are credited to Percy Montross in the 1880s, and the melody is possibly German or Mexican. Today singers of all ages make up their own versions—like "O My Monster Frankenstein" or "Found a Peanut."

Try to sing without laughing

1. In a cav - ern, in a can - yon, Ex - ca - vat - ing for a

mine, Lived a min - er, for - ty - nin - er, And his daugh - ter, Clem - en -

CHORUS

tine. O my dar - ling, O my dar - ling, O my dar - ling Clem - en -

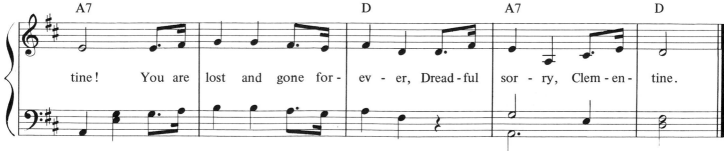

tine! You are lost and gone for - ev - er, Dread - ful sor - ry, Clem - en - tine.

2. Light she was and like a fairy,
        and her shoes were number nine.
   Herring boxes without topses, sandals were
        for Clementine.
                    CHORUS

3. Drove her ducklings to the water
        every morning just at nine.
   Hit her foot against a splinter, fell into
        the foaming brine.
                    CHORUS

4. Ruby lips above the water,
        blowing bubbles soft and fine.
   But, alas! I was no swimmer, so I lost
        my Clementine.
                    CHORUS

5. In a churchyard near the canyon,
        where the myrtle does entwine,
   There grow roses and other posies fertilized
        by Clementine.
                    CHORUS

6. In my dreams she still does haunt me,
        robed in garments soaked in brine.
   Though in life I used to hug her, now she's dead,
        I draw the line.
                    CHORUS

7. How I missed her, how I missed her,
        how I missed my Clementine,
   Till I kissed her little sister, and forgot
        my Clementine.
                    CHORUS

8. Listen, Girl Scouts, heed the warning
        to this tragic tale of mine;
   Artificial respiration could have saved
        my Clementine.
                    CHORUS

THE COWBOY'S LAMENT
◖ or, The Streets of Laredo

TEXAS

Cowboys fancied themselves carefree and glamorous, but the other side of the coin was death at the hands of outlaws, Indians, or even each other. So many died fighting—"with their boots on"—that the local cemetery was called Boot Hill. Here a young cowboy from Laredo, Texas, speaks his last words as he lies wrapped in a white sheet and his companions carry him in a "dead march" to the cemetery. The tune derives from an old Irish air, but this was at one time the most widely sung ballad in the American West.

Like a dirge

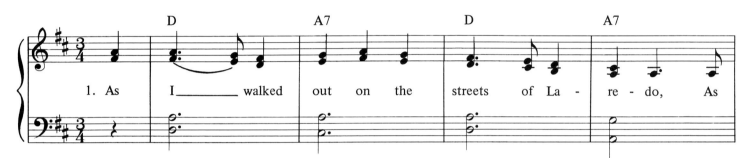

1. As I _____ walked out on the streets of La - re - do, As

I walked out in La - re - do one day, I spied a young cow-boy all

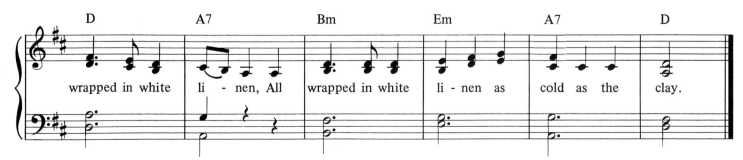

wrapped in white li - nen, All wrapped in white li - nen as cold as the clay.

2. "I see by your outfit that you are a cowboy."
These words he did say as I boldly walked by.
"Come sit down beside me and hear my sad story;
I was shot in the breast and I know I must die."

3. "It was once in the saddle I used to go dashing,
With no one as quick on the trigger as I.
I sat in a card game in back of the barroom,
Got shot in the back, and today I must die."

4. "Let sixteen gamblers come handle my coffin,
   Let sixteen cowboys come sing me a song.
   Just take me to Boot Hill and lay the sod o'er me,
   For I'm a young cowboy and I know I've done wrong."

5. "Oh, beat the drum slowly and play the fife lowly,
   And play the dead march as you carry my pall.
   Put bunches of roses all over my coffin,
   Roses to deaden the clods as they fall."

6. "Go gather around you a crowd of young cowboys
   And tell them the story of this, my sad fate.
   Tell one and the other before they go further
   To stop their wild roving before it's too late."

7. "Go fetch me a cup, a cup of cold water,
   To cool my parched lips," the cowboy then said.
   Before I returned, his brave spirit had left him
   And gone to its Maker—the cowboy was dead.

8. We beat the drum slowly and played the fife lowly,
   And bitterly wept as we bore him along,
   For we all loved our comrade, so brave, young, and handsome.
   We all loved our comrade although he'd done wrong.

THE CRAWDAD SONG

SOUTHERN

A crawdad is a Southern crayfish—a tasty crustacean that looks like a miniature gray lobster. You go fishing for crawdads in creeks, and if you catch some, you eat them or use them to catch larger fish. In the hottest part of summer the streams dry out, the crawdads scramble up the banks—and you can't do much besides sing songs about them. This one derives from children's play-party dances, and songs sung by the workers building embankments (levees) to prevent flooding of the Mississippi River in the South.

Breezy

1. You get a line and I'll get a pole,___ hon-ey.

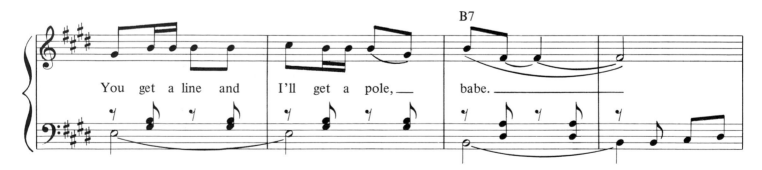

You get a line and I'll get a pole,___ babe.

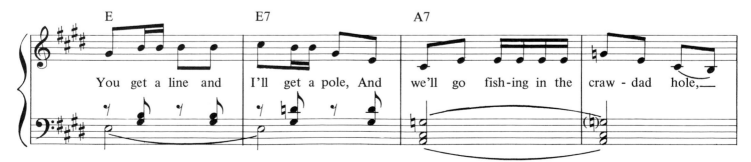

You get a line and I'll get a pole, And we'll go fish-ing in the craw-dad hole,___

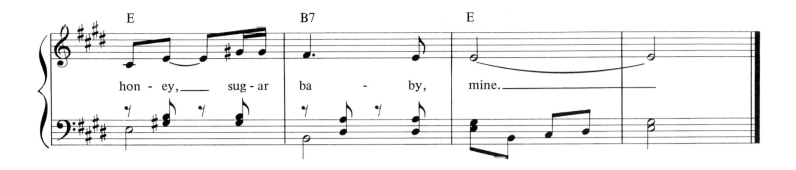

hon - ey,____ sug - ar ba - by, mine.____

2. What you gonna do when the stream runs dry, honey?
   What you gonna do when the stream runs dry, babe?
   What you gonna do when the stream runs dry?
   Sit on the bank and watch the crawdads die, honey,
        sugar baby, mine.

3. What you gonna do when the crawdads die, honey?
   What you gonna do when the crawdads die, babe?
   What you gonna do when the crawdads die?
   Sit on the bank until I cry, honey,
        sugar baby, mine.

4. Yonder comes a man with a sack on his back, honey.
   Oh, yonder comes a man with a sack on his back, babe.
   Yonder comes a man with a sack on his back,
   And he's got all the crawdads he can pack, honey,
        sugar baby, mine.

5. That fellow fall down and he bust his sack, honey.
   That man fall down and he bust his sack, babe.
   That man fall down and he bust his sack.
   Hey, look at all the crawdads backing back, honey,
        sugar baby, mine.

6. Well, look at that crawdad crawling around, honey.
   Oh, look at that crawdad crawling around, babe.
   Oh, look at that crawdad crawling around.
   Why, he's the Mayor of Crawdad Town, honey,
        sugar baby, mine.

25

DOWN BY THE RIVERSIDE
ℂ or, Ain't Gonna Study War No More

SOUTHERN

Associated with the 1960s civil-rights movement and Vietnam War protests, this black spiritual is a plea for justice, as well as a song about dying and going to heaven. A hundred years ago slaves used it as a work song. The "riverside" meant the local stream where slaves met on Sundays for religious services, and also symbolized the river Jordan, where, in the Bible, Jesus was baptized. Beyond Jordan lay the Promised Land, and beyond the rivers that the slaves knew (the Ohio, Mississippi, or Missouri) lay the slavery-free North.

With a strong beat

I ain't gon-na stu-dy war no more, I ain't gon-na

stu-dy war no more. I ain't gon-na stu-dy_____ war no

1. more._____ I ain't gon-na **2.** more._____

2. I'm gonna lay down my burden there, etc.

3. I'm gonna walk with the Prince of Peace, etc.

4. I'm gonna meet my old father, etc.

5. I'm gonna meet my old mother, etc.

6. Yes, I'm gonna shake hands around the world, etc.

DOWN IN THE VALLEY

Descending from an old British air, this song dates from pioneer days in the Appalachian Mountains. Jailed in Birmingham, Alabama, the singer feels isolated from his loved one. The rugged hills and valleys between them intensify these feelings of separation, and his only means of communication is the mail. His mournful message has been sung as a cowboy tune, a love ballad, a country-music song, and a hit of the 1960s folk revival. The jail's name can be changed to suit your locale.

Debonair

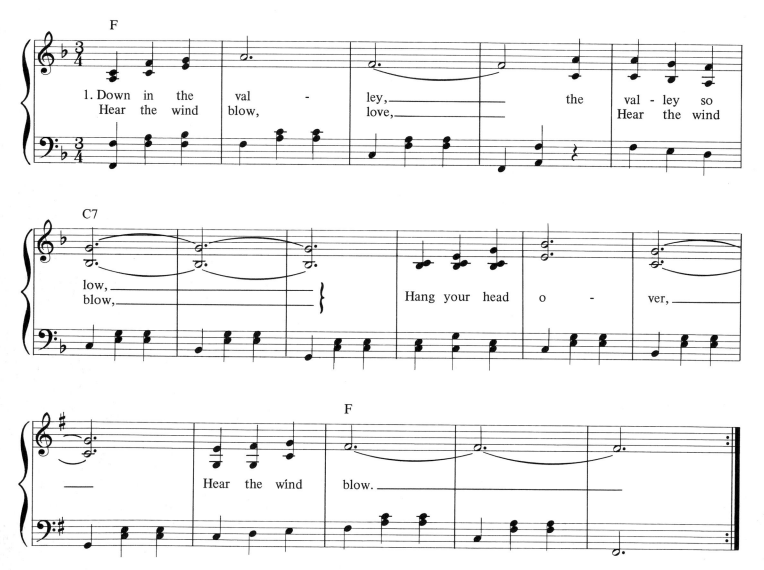

2. Roses love sunshine, violets love dew,
   Angels in heaven know I love you.
   Know I love you, dear, know I love you,
   Angels in heaven know I love you.

3. Write me a letter, send it by mail,
   Send it in care of Birmingham jail.
   Birmingham jail, love, Birmingham jail,
   Send it in care of Birmingham jail.

4. This gloomy prison is far from you, dear,
   But not forever, I'm out in a year.
   Out in a year, love, out in a year,
   But not forever, I'm out in a year.

5. I make this promise to go straight and true,
   And for a lifetime to love only you.
   Love only you, dear, love only you,
   And for a lifetime to love only you.

THE ERIE CANAL
or, I've Got a Mule

New York State

The Erie Canal, a man-made waterway connecting the Atlantic Ocean with the Great Lakes, opened up the Midwest to communication and trade with Eastern states in 1825. Barges drawn by mules or horses walking on a towpath parallel to the canal kept up a steady traffic on the peaceful waters. For the navigating drivers, songs helped to head off sleepiness. The cry of "Low bridge!" signaled a town coming up with a walkway over the canal, making it advisable to duck. By 1850 efficient railroads were supplanting the barges, rendering the canal obsolete — but not this ode to it.

With a blues beat

1. I've got a mule, her name is Sal,
She's a good old work-er and a good old pal,
Fif-teen miles on the

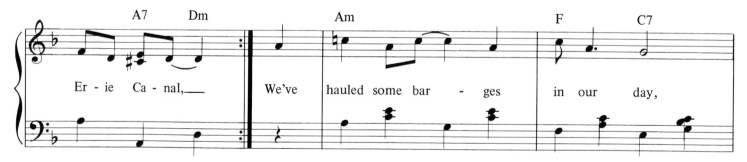

Er - ie Ca - nal,___ We've hauled some bar - ges in our day,

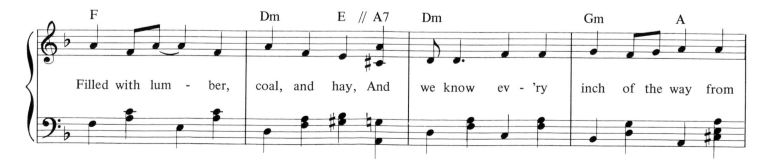

Filled with lum - ber, coal, and hay, And we know ev - 'ry inch of the way from

CHORUS

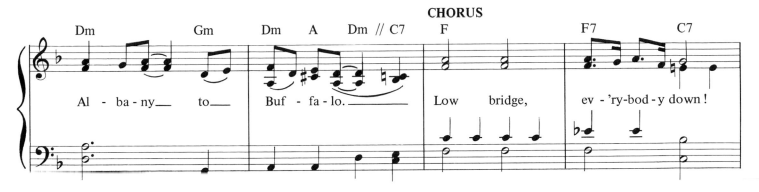

Al - ba - ny___ to___ Buf - fa - lo.___ Low bridge, ev - 'ry-bod-y down!

Low bridge, for we're com - ing to a town! And you'll al - ways know your neigh-bor, you'll

al - ways know your pal, If you've ev - er nav - i - ga - ted on the Er - ie Ca - nal.___

2. We'd better get along on our way, old pal.
   Fifteen miles on the Erie Canal.
   'Cause you bet your life I'd never part with Sal.
   Fifteen miles on the Erie Canal.
   Get up there, mule, here comes a lock;
   We'll make Rome 'bout six o'clock.
   One more trip and back we'll go,
   Right back home to Buffalo.
   CHORUS

3. Oh, where would I be if I lost my pal?
   Fifteen miles on the Erie Canal.
   Oh, I'd like to see a mule as good as Sal.
   Fifteen miles on the Erie Canal.
   A friend of mine once got her sore;
   Now he's got a broken jaw,
   'Cause she let fly with her iron toe
   And kicked him into Buffalo.
   CHORUS

FOLLOW THE DRINKING GOURD

SOUTHERN

These pre—Civil War lyrics gave enslaved blacks directions for the local branch of the Underground Railroad: the secret path leading to safe places in the North. The constellation of stars known as the Big Dipper is shaped like a gourd shell. It indicated the right direction, as did the trail of distinctive marks on dead trees left by a white sailor named Peg Leg Joe (the "old man"). He described three rivers—the Tombigbee, the Tennessee, and the Ohio—that led to freedom; traveling at night was safest; and the least dangerous season was spring, when "the first quail calls."

With vigor

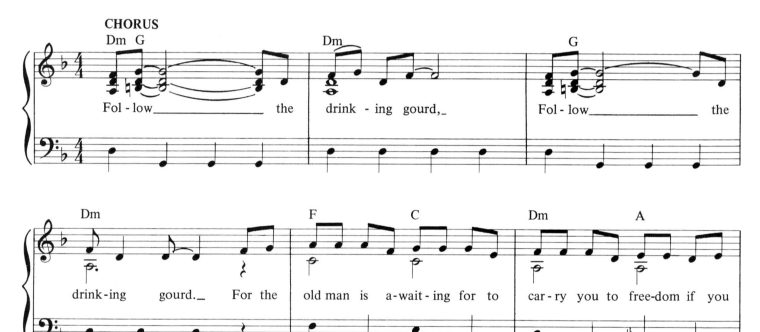

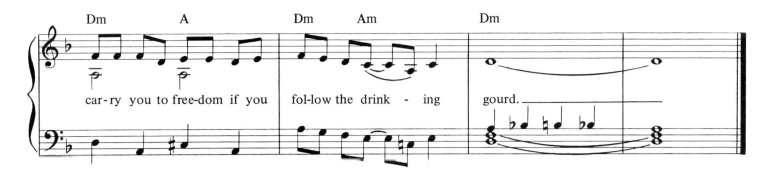

car-ry you to free-dom if you | fol-low the drink - ing | gourd. ____

CHORUS

2. Now the riverbank makes a very good road.
   The dead trees will show you the way.
   Left foot, peg foot, traveling on.
   Follow the drinking gourd.

CHORUS

3. Now the river ends between two hills.
   Follow the drinking gourd.
   There's another river on the other side.
   Follow the drinking gourd.

CHORUS

4. When the great big river meets the little river,
   Follow the drinking gourd.
   For the old man is a-waiting for to carry you to freedom.
   Follow the drinking gourd.

THE FOX
(Went Out on a Chilly Night)

Farmers traditionally see a fox as an enemy that gobbles valuable farm animals and precious crops. But from a certain point of view (namely, the fox's), the sly fox is a hero. Popular since the United States was a group of thirteen British colonies, this tale of one fox's triumph derives from an old English folk song.

Mischievously

1. The fox went out on a chill-y night,— Prayed for the moon to give him light,— He'd

man-y a mile to go that night be - fore he reached the town - o, town - o,

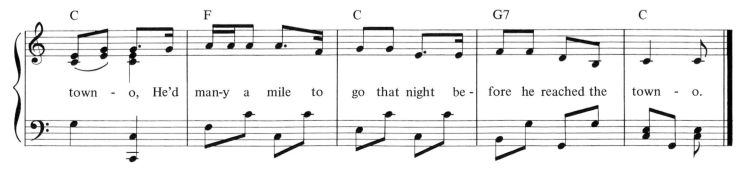

town - o, He'd man-y a mile to go that night be - fore he reached the town - o.

34

2. He ran till he came to a great big bin;
   The ducks and the geese were kept therein.
   "A couple of you will grease my chin
   Before I leave this town-o, town-o, town-o.
   A couple of you will grease my chin
   Before I leave this town-o."

3. He grabbed the gray goose by the neck
   And threw a duck across his back.
   He didn't mind their "Quack, quack, quack"
   And their legs all dangling down-o, etc.

4. Old Mother Pitter-Patter jumped out of bed;
   Out of the window she cocked her head,
   Said, "Get up, John! The gray goose is gone,
   And the fox is in the town-o," etc.

5. John, he went to the top of the hill,
   And he blew on his horn both loud and shrill.
   The fox, he said, "I'd better leave with my kill;
   He'll soon be on my trail-o," etc.

6. He ran till he came to his cozy den,
   And there were the little ones, eight, nine, ten.
   They said, "Daddy, you'd better go back again,
   'Cause it must be a mighty fine town-o," etc.

7. Then the fox and his wife, without any strife,
   They cut up the goose with a fork and a knife.
   They never had such a supper in their life,
   And the little ones chewed on the bones-o, etc.

FREIGHT TRAIN

Elizabeth Cotten's (1893–1987) older brother had to leave the house before she could sneak in some practice on his guitar. By the time she was twelve, around 1912, she had bought her own guitar for $3.75 — five months' wages as a domestic worker. When she played guitar and sang with her brothers, each had his or her own special song. "Freight Train" was her song. It was inspired by the train running near her home, in Chapel Hill, North Carolina.

Mellow

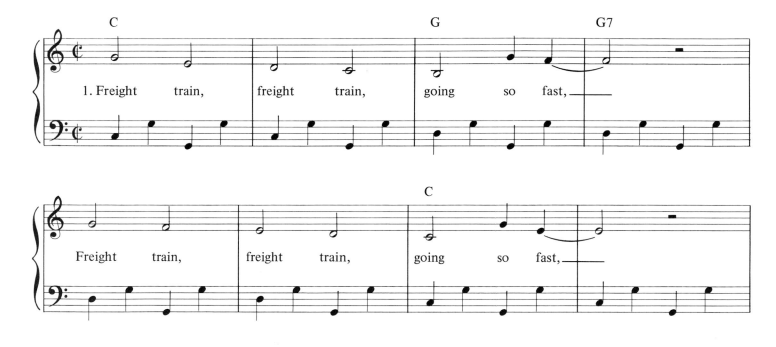

1. Freight train, freight train, going so fast,

Freight train, freight train, going so fast,

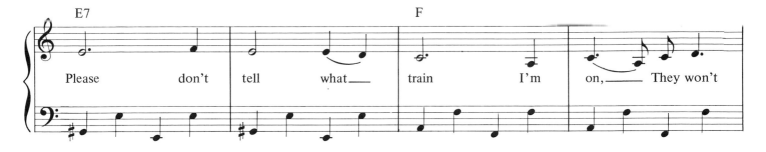

Please   don't   tell   what___   train   I'm   on,___   They won't

know   what___   route   I've   gone.

2. When I'm dead and in my grave,
   No more good times here I'll crave.
   Place a stone at my head and feet;
   Tell my friends that I've gone to sleep.

3. When I die, Lord, bury me deep,
   Way down on old Chestnut Street,
   So I can hear old Number Nine
   As she goes roaring by.

4. Repeat first verse.

THE FROZEN LOGGER

Words and music: JAMES STEVENS

A 1929 radio program about the legendary lumberjack Paul Bunyan inspired this braggarts' waltz from the Northwest logging country. A real-life lumberjack's life did demand strength, but the logger here is so *unbelievably* macho that he can survive just about anything. For those who cut timber to clear land and build houses, a song like this was useful: The falls of the ax could be timed to fit the breaks after each line.

With flair

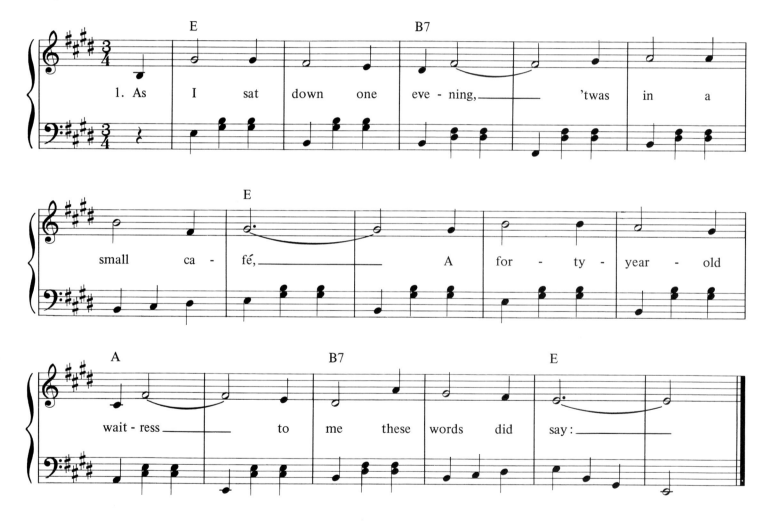

2. I see you are a logger and not a common bum,
   For no one but a logger stirs his coffee with his thumb.

3. My lover was a logger; there's none like him today.
   If you poured whiskey on it, he would eat a bale of hay.

4. He never shaved the whiskers from off his horny hide,
   But drove them in with a hammer and bit them off inside.

5. My lover came to see me; 'twas on a freezing day.
   He held me in a fond embrace that broke three vertebrae.

6. He kissed me when we parted, so hard he broke my jaw.
   I could not speak to tell him he forgot his mackinaw.

7. I saw my logger lover sauntering through the snow,
   A-going gaily homeward at forty-eight below.

8. Well, the weather it tried to freeze him; it tried its level best.
   At one hundred degrees below zero, he buttoned up his vest.

9. It froze clean through to China; it froze to the stars above.
   And at one thousand degrees below zero, it froze my logger love.

10. And so I lost my lover, and to this café I come,
    And here I wait till someone stirs his coffee with his thumb.

GIT ALONG, LITTLE DOGIES

WESTERN

Dogies (pronounced *dō-gēs*) weren't dogs, but cows. And they weren't little: Some weighed over a thousand pounds. Between 1870 and 1890 some twelve million cows were taken from Texas to new grazing ground in Wyoming, to be fattened up and sold as food in Idaho. The cowboys spent long dusty days and cold sleepless nights trying to keep an endless unpredictable parade together. The melody of this cowboy song is vaguely Irish, but "Whoopee ti yi yo" is strictly American: a sharp rhythmic cry to energize sluggish cows without frightening them.

Loping

1. As I was a-walk-ing one morn-ing for plea-sure, I
hat was thrown back and his spurs were a - jing - ling, And

spied a cow-punch-er a - rid-ing a - lone. His
as he ap-proached he was sing-ing this

CHORUS

song: Whoop-ee ti yi yo, git a - long, lit - tle

do - gies, It's your mis - for - tune and none of my

own. Whoop-ee ti yi yo, git a - long, lit - tle

do - gies, You know that Wy - om - ing will be your new home.

2. It's early in spring that we round up the dogies;
   We mark them and brand them and bob off their tails;
   We round up the horses, load up the chuck wagon,
   And then throw the dogies upon the long trail.
   CHORUS

3. Your mothers were raised away down in Texas,
   Where the jimson weed and the sandburs grow.
   Now we'll fill you up on prickly pear and cactus,
   Till you are all ready for the trail to Idaho.
   CHORUS

4. When night comes on, we herd them on the bedground;
   These little dogies that roll on so slow.
   Roll up the herd and cut out the strays,
   And roll the little dogies that never rolled before.
   CHORUS

5. Some boys a-hit this old cattle trail for pleasure;
   That's where they get it most awfully wrong.
   I wish they could tell you the troubles they give us
   As we go rolling these dogies along.
   CHORUS

6. It's whooping and yelling and driving the dogies;
   Oh, how I wish that they would go on!
   It's whooping and punching and go on, little dogies,
   For you know Wyoming's gonna be your new home!
   CHORUS

GO TELL AUNT RHODY

So ingrained is this short, sweet song in American folk history that no one knows exactly where it started—possibly as a play-party song. Play-parties were New England teenagers' way around the Puritan restrictions against dancing and playing musical instruments. Singing games to the accompaniment of clapping hands *were* permitted and soon became the main form of entertainment in all the colonies. The aunt's name is Rhody, Patsy, Dinah, and so on, depending on the locale; you can substitute the name of an aunt you know.

Nimble

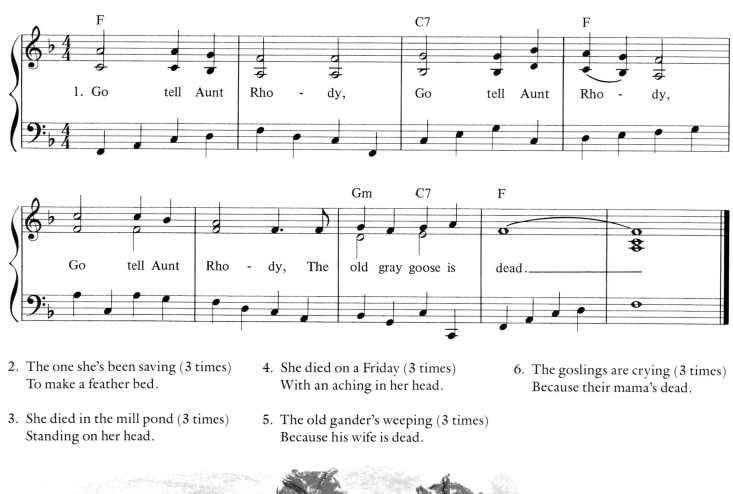

2. The one she's been saving (**3 times**)
   To make a feather bed.

3. She died in the mill pond (**3 times**)
   Standing on her head.

4. She died on a Friday (**3 times**)
   With an aching in her head.

5. The old gander's weeping (**3 times**)
   Because his wife is dead.

6. The goslings are crying (**3 times**)
   Because their mama's dead.

GO TELL IT ON THE MOUNTAIN

SOUTHERN

This traditional black spiritual has a Christmas theme, though it's popular all year round. During the 1960s, civil rights marchers adapted it as a protest song, and the last line of the chorus became "And let my people go." The song was a hit single for Peter, Paul, and Mary in 1964.

Boisterous

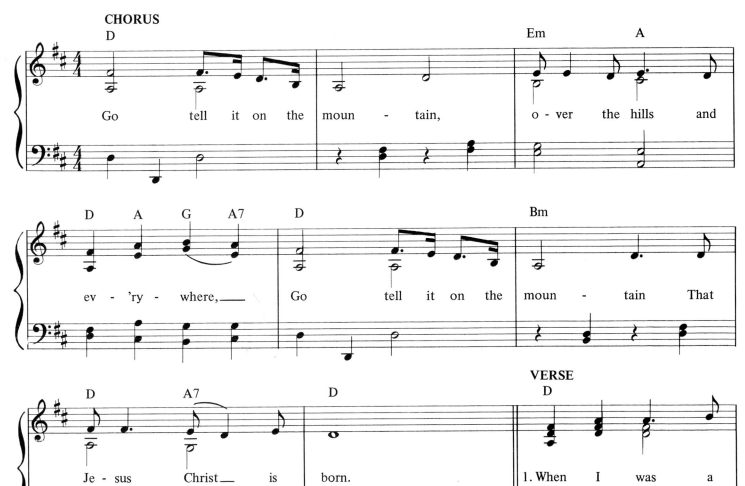

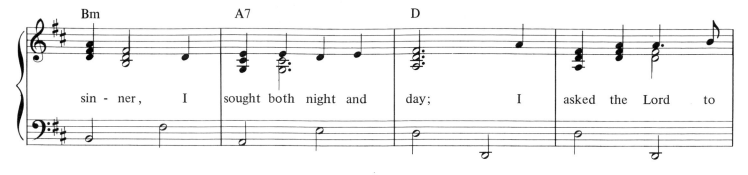

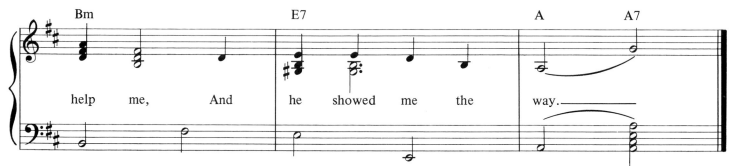

sin - ner, I sought both night and day; I asked the Lord to

help me, And he showed me the way._____

2. The shepherds kept their watching
   O'er silent flocks by night,
   When lo! throughout the heavens
   There shone a holy light.
   CHORUS

3. The shepherds feared and trembled,
   When high above the earth
   Rang out an angel chorus
   To hail our Savior's birth.
   CHORUS

4. It was in a lowly manger
   That Jesus Christ was born;
   And God sent out salvation
   That bright and glorious morn.
   CHORUS

GOING TO THE ZOO

Words and music: TOM PAXTON

Born in Chicago in 1937, Tom Paxton grew up in Oklahoma and was influenced musically by fellow Oklahoman Woody Guthrie and by Pete Seeger and Jacques Brel. He is especially known for—among his fifteen hundred songs—"The Last Thing on My Mind," "The Marvelous Toy," and this, which says everything there is to say about the zoo.

Cute

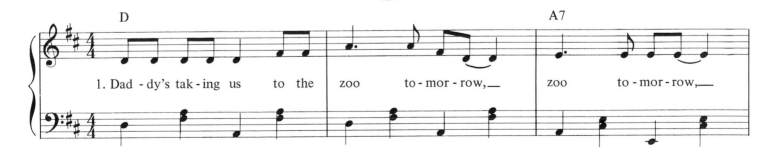

We can — stay all day. We're go-ing to the zoo, zoo,

zoo. How a-bout you, you, you? You can come

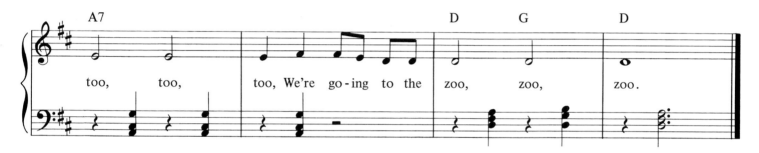

too, too, too, We're go-ing to the zoo, zoo, zoo.

2. See the elephant with the long trunk swingin',
   Great big ears and long trunk swingin',
   Sniffing up peanuts with the long trunk swingin'—
   We can stay all day.
   CHORUS

3. See all the monkeys scritch, scritch, scratchin',
   Jumping all around and scritch, scritch, scratchin',
   Hanging by their long tails scritch, scritch, scratchin'—
   We can stay all day.
   CHORUS

4. Big black bear all huff huff a-puffin',
   Coat's too heavy, he's huff huff a-puffin',
   Don't get too near the huff huff a-puffin'—
   Or you won't stay all day.
   CHORUS

5. Seals in the pool all honk, honk, honkin',
   Catching fish and honk, honk, honkin',
   Little seals honk, honk, honkin'—
   We can stay all day.
   CHORUS

6. *(Slower)* We stayed all day and I'm gettin' sleepy,
   Sitting in the car getting sleep, sleep, sleepy,
   Home already and I'm sleep, sleep, sleepy—
   We have stayed all day.
   We've been to the zoo, zoo, zoo,
   So have you, you, you,
   You came too, too, too,
   We've been to the zoo, zoo, zoo.

7. *(Faster)* Mama's taking us to the zoo tomorrow, etc.

GOOD NIGHT, IRENE

Words and music: HUDDIE LEDBETTER and JOHN LOMAX

While a prisoner at the Louisiana State Prison in Angola in 1936, Huddie Ledbetter (better known as Leadbelly), a twelve-string guitar wizard, recorded this waltz with John Lomax, a well-known musicologist. Leadbelly (1885–1949) learned the song from his uncle and said that there was a real Irene at one time. Many people have recorded it since, from the Weavers (who sold almost 2 million copies) and Raffi to Brian Wilson of the Beach Boys.

Crooning

married,_____ Me and my wife set - tled down,_____

_____ Now me and my wife___ have part - ed,_____ I'm gon - na

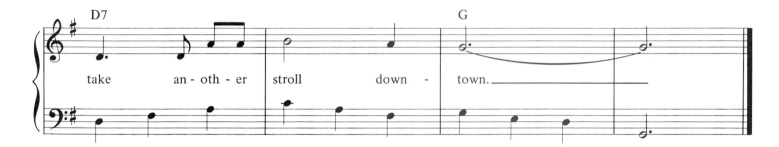

take an - oth - er stroll down - town._____

LEAD BELLY

CHORUS
2. Sometimes I live in the country;
   Sometimes I live in town.
   Sometimes I take a great notion
   To jump into the river and drown.

CHORUS
3. Stop rambling, stop your gambling;
   Stop staying out at night.
   Go home to your wife and your family;
   Stay there by your fireside bright.
                          CHORUS

HOME ON THE RANGE

KANSAS

It's said that Brewster Higley, an eccentric Kansas doctor, and Dan Kelly, a guitar-playing carpenter, wrote this song in 1873. Their hymn to wide-open spaces romanticizes what was in fact a harsh life. They called it "My Western Home" and nowhere included the words "home on the range." But it mutated into "the cowboys' national anthem," becoming the favorite song of Franklin D. Roosevelt and Kansas's official state song.

Like cowboys around a campfire

1. Oh, give me a home where the buf - fa - lo roam, Where the

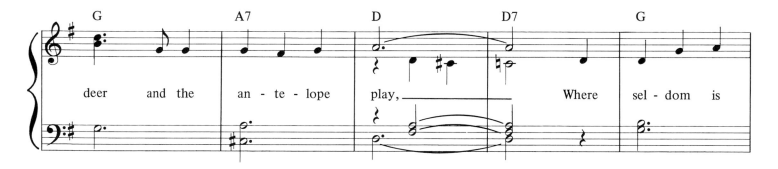

deer and the an - te - lope play, _____ Where sel - dom is

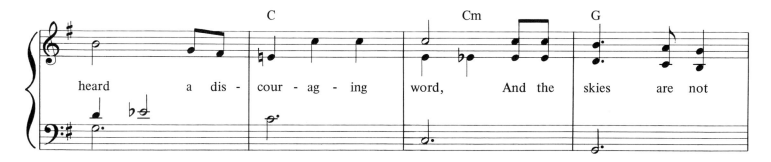

heard a dis - cour - ag - ing word, And the skies are not

cloud - y all day. _____ **CHORUS** Home, home on the

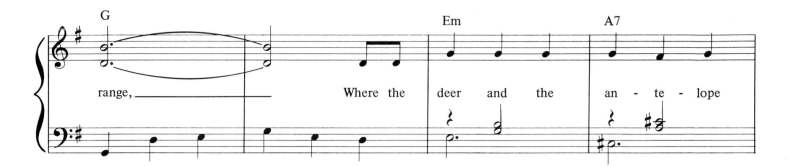

range, _____ Where the deer and the an - te - lope

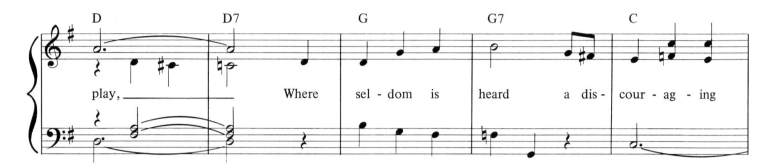

play, _____ Where sel - dom is heard a dis - cour - ag - ing

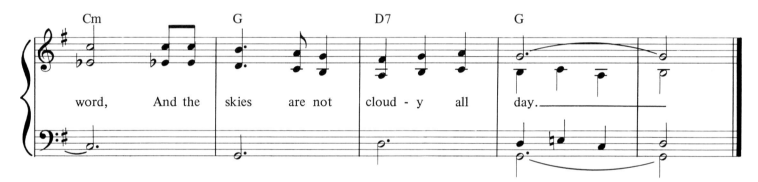

word, And the skies are not cloud - y all day. _____

2. Oh, give me a land where the bright diamond sand
   Flows leisurely down the stream;
   Where the graceful white swan goes gliding along
   Like a maid in a heavenly dream.

   CHORUS

3. How often at night, when the heavens are bright
   With the light from the glittering stars,
   Have I stood there amazed and asked as I gazed
   If their glory exceeds that of ours.

   CHORUS

4. Where the air is so pure, the zephyrs so free,
   The breezes so balmy and light,
   That I would not exchange my home on the range
   For all of the cities so bright.

   CHORUS

I RIDE AN OLD PAINT

TEXAS / OKLAHOMA

Not many songs could soothe a restless herd of cattle *and* get people waltzing at Western dances. The cowboy expressions here call for some translation: The cowboy rides his favorite spotted horse and leads another; he's on his way to a Montana rodeo, where he's going to wrestle steers; his horses, sore from the long journey, feed in the ravines; but they're still full of pep, and the cowboy wishes his cattle would follow their "fiery and snuffy" lead.

Like a lullaby

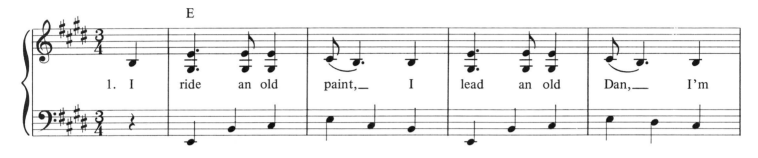

1. I ride an old paint,__ I lead an old Dan,__ I'm

goin' to Mon-tan-a to throw the houl-i-han. They feed in the

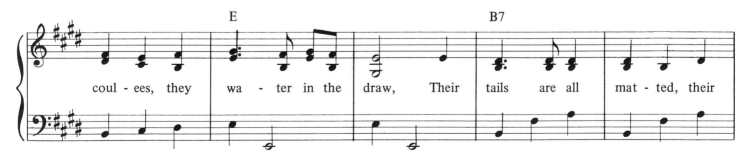

coul-ees, they wa-ter in the draw, Their tails are all mat-ted, their

CHORUS

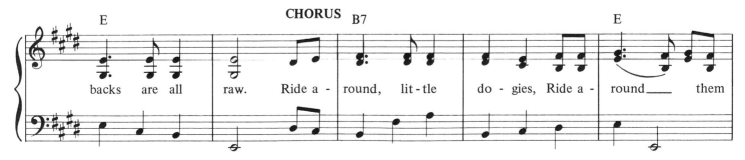

backs are all raw. Ride a-round, lit-tle do-gies, Ride a-round__ them

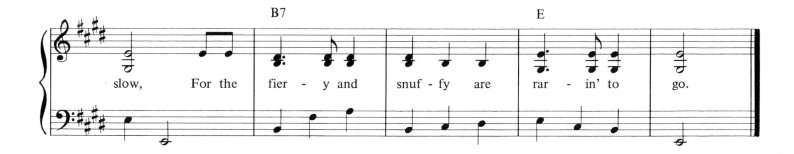

slow, For the fier — y and snuf - fy are rar — in' to go.

2. I've worked in your town, I've worked on your farm,
   And all I got to show is the muscle in my arm,
   Blisters on my feet, and the callous on my hand.
   I'm going to Montana to throw the houlihan.
                                    CHORUS

3. When I die, don't bury me at all;
   Put me on my pony and lead him from his stall,
   Tie my bones to his back, turn our faces to the west,
   And we'll ride the prairie that we love the best.
                                    CHORUS

I WAS BORN ABOUT
TEN THOUSAND YEARS AGO

TRADITIONAL AMERICAN

Tellers of tall tales say: If you're going to tell a lie, you might as well make it a whopper. This bragging song from the late 1800s manages to span Milwaukee, Tennessee, Christopher Columbus, President George Washington, General Joseph Hooker from the Civil War—and also bits of tall tales, Bible stories, folklore, the history of the world, and total nonsense. If you've ever made up a limerick, you know how to make up your own verses here. (Noel Stookey, of the singing group Peter, Paul, and Mary, adopted the name "Paul" after the third line of this song.)

Sassy

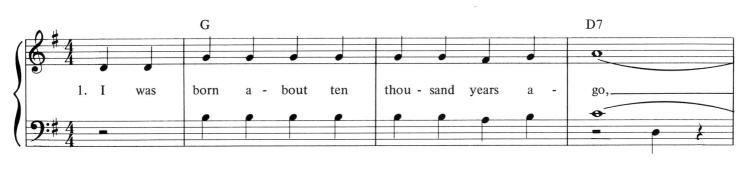

1. I was born a-bout ten thou-sand years a - go,

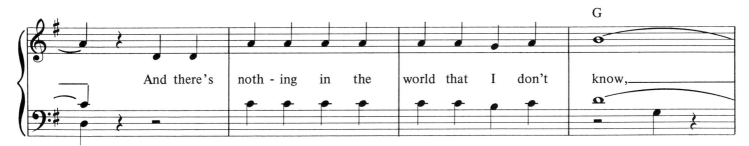

And there's noth-ing in the world that I don't know,

54

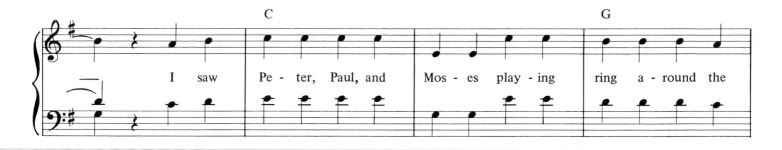

C   G

I saw Pe - ter, Paul, and Mos - es play - ing ring a - round the

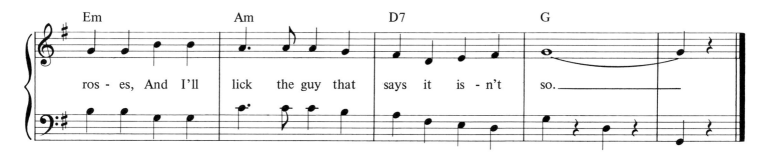

Em   Am   D7   G

ros - es, And I'll lick the guy that says it is - n't so.

2. I saw Satan when he looked the garden o'er,
   I saw Eve and Adam driven from the door,
   And behind the bushes peeping,
   Saw the apple they were eating,
   And I'll swear that I'm the guy that ate the core.

3. I taught Samson how to use his mighty hands,
   Showed Columbus how to reach this happy land,
   And for Pharaoh's little kiddies
   I built all the pyramiddies,
   And to Sahara carried all the sand.

4. I taught Solomon his little ABC's,
   I was the first one ate Limburger cheese,
   And while sailing down the bay
   With Methuselah one day,
   I saved his flowing whiskers from the breeze.

5. Queen Elizabeth, she fell in love with me,
   We were married in Milwaukee secretly,
   But I snuck around and shook her,
   And I went with General Hooker
   To shoot mosquitoes down in Tennessee.

6. I remember when the country had a king,
   I saw Cleopatra pawn her wedding ring,
   And I saw the flags a-flying
   When George Washington stopped lying
   On the night when Patti first began to sing.

7. I saw Samson when he laid the village cold,
   I saw Daniel tame the lions in their hold,
   I helped build the tower of Babel
   Up as high as they were able,
   And there's lots of other things I haven't told.

IF I HAD A HAMMER
or, The Hammer Song

Words and music: LEE HAYS and PETE SEEGER

Lee Hays and Pete Seeger, cofounders of the Weavers folk-singing group during the late 1940s, wrote this anthem about the power each individual has to change the world. At a meeting of People's Songs—a sort of clearinghouse for folk musicians— they kept themselves amused by passing a sheet of paper back and forth, piecing it all together. The third verse inspired the name of the magazine *Sing Out!,* which featured the song in its first issue and has published hundreds of folk songs since.

With conviction

I'd _____ ham-mer out   love   be-tween   my   broth-ers   and   my   sis - ters,

All _____ o - ver this land. _____

2. If I had a bell, I'd ring it in the morning,
   I'd ring it in the evening, all over this land.
   I'd ring out danger, I'd ring out a warning,
   I'd ring out love between my brothers and my sisters,
   All over this land.

3. If I had a song, I'd sing it in the morning,
   I'd sing it in the evening, all over this land.
   I'd sing out danger, I'd sing out a warning,
   I'd sing out love between my brothers and my sisters,
   All over this land.

4. Well, I got a hammer, and I've got a bell,
   And I've got a song to sing, all over this land.
   It's the hammer of justice, it's the bell of freedom,
   It's the song about love between my brothers and my sisters,
   All over this land.

I'VE BEEN WORKING ON
THE RAILROAD

Almost 100,000 miles of railroad track were in operation by 1880, stitching
America together. This sturdy anthem of the railroad workers may have descended
from an old Irish hymn or from "I've Been Working on the Levee," sung by gangs
building levees on the Mississippi River. Dinah was perhaps a train or else a real
woman, with "blow your horn" meaning "call me for lunch." "Someone's in the
Kitchen with Dinah" was actually a separate song, but because of the "Dinah"
connection, it came to be linked with this one.

Pell-mell

I've been work-ing on the rail - road all the live - long

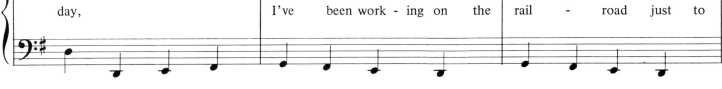

day, I've been work-ing on the rail - road just to

pass the time a - way. Don't you hear the whis - tle

blow - ing?   Rise   up so ear - ly in the   morn,

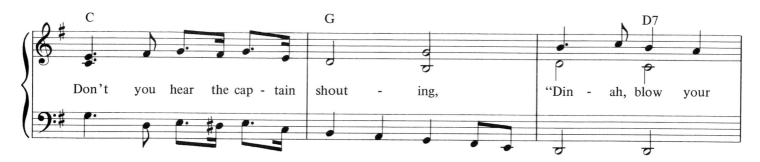

Don't   you hear   the cap - tain   shout - - ing,   "Din - ah, blow your

horn!"?   Din - ah, won't you blow,   Din - ah, won't you blow,

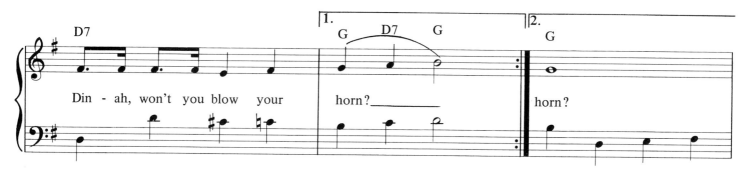

Din - ah, won't you blow   your   horn?_____   horn?

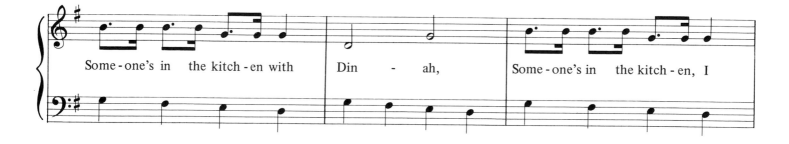

Some - one's in   the kitch - en with   Din - - ah,   Some - one's in   the kitch - en, I

know._____ Some - one's in the kitch - en with Din - ah,

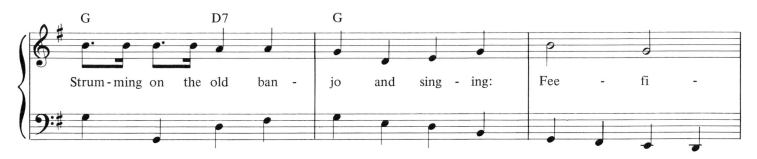

Strum - ming on the old ban - jo and sing - ing: Fee - fi -

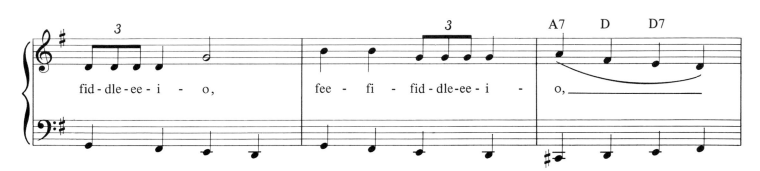

fid - dle - ee - i - o, fee - fi - fid - dle - ee - i - o,_____

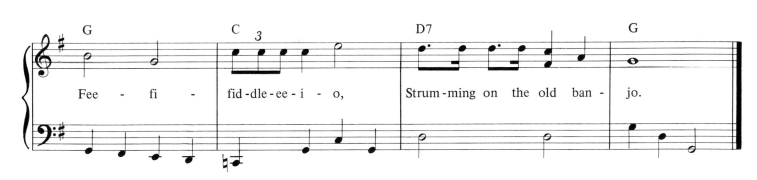

Fee - fi - fid - dle - ee - i - o, Strum - ming on the old ban - jo.

JESSE JAMES

MISSOURI

Thought to have been written by a convict named Billy Gashade, this ballad celebrates perhaps the most famous American outlaw ever. Jesse James (1847–1882) enjoyed a reputation as a "good" bad guy who stole from the rich and gave to the poor, had style, and was kind to women. He had retired to St. Joseph, Missouri, under the assumed name of Thomas Howard, and was hanging a picture when he was shot in the back. Robert Ford, a member of James's own gang, collected the $10,000 reward and months later died in a fight over a card game. By that time Jesse James was considered such a hero that seventeen men were claiming to be him, still alive.

Animated

chil - dren, they were brave, But that dir - ty lit - tle cow - ard that

shot Mis - ter How - ard, He laid poor Jes - se in his grave.

2. It was on a Saturday night and the moon was shining bright,
They robbed the Glendale train.
And the people they did say, for many miles away,
'Twas the outlaws Frank and Jesse James.

CHORUS

3. Oh, Jesse was a man, a friend of the poor;
He'd never rob a mother or a child.
And with his brother Frank he robbed the Chicago bank
And stopped the Glendale train.

CHORUS

4. Well, it was Robert Ford, that dirty little coward;
I wonder how he does feel.
For he ate of Jesse's bread and he slept in Jesse's bed,
Then he laid Jesse James in his grave.

CHORUS

5. The people held their breath when they learned of
Jesse's death;
They wondered how he ever came to fall.
Robert Ford, it was a fact, shot Jesse in the back
While Jesse hung a picture on the wall.

CHORUS

6. Well, this song was made by Billy Gashade
As soon as the news did arrive.
He said there was no man with the law in his hand
Who could take Jesse James when alive.

CHORUS

JOE HILL

Words and music: ALFRED HAYES and EARL ROBINSON

Joe Hill (1879–1915) was a labor activist and songwriter who traveled across America, helping workers organize into unions and writing what many consider America's first protest songs. He was convicted of a murder he swore he didn't commit, and executed by a Utah firing squad despite pleas from President Woodrow Wilson and sympathizers around the world. First performed around a campfire, this song later had its largest audience when Joan Baez sang it at the Woodstock Music Festival in 1969. For the next twenty years it was her most requested song.

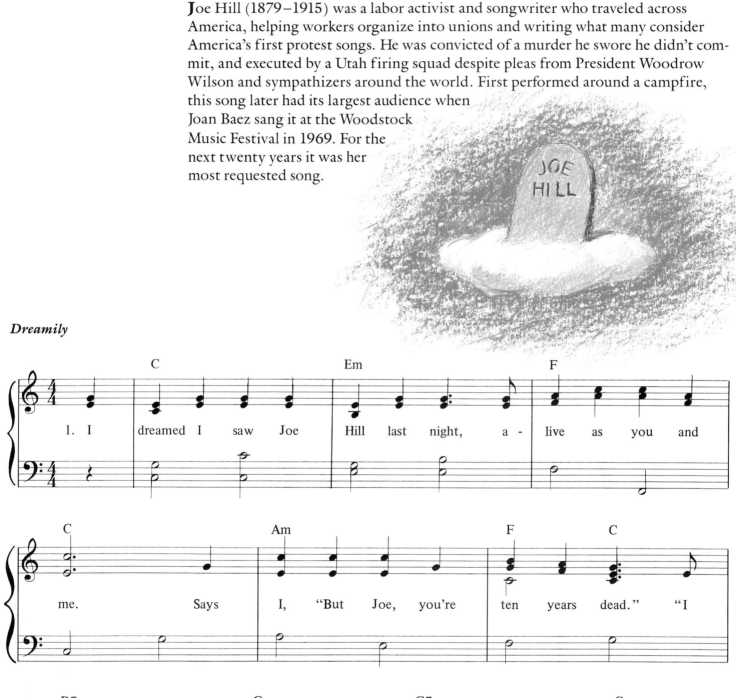

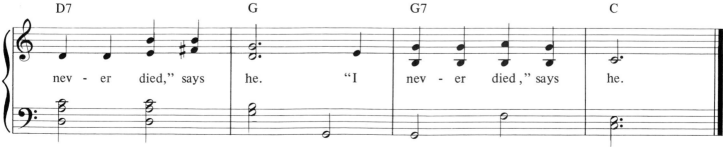

2. "In Salt Lake, Joe," says I to him, him standing by my bed,
   "They framed you on a murder charge." Says Joe, "But I ain't dead."
   Says Joe, "But I ain't dead."

3. "The copper bosses killed you, Joe, they shot you, Joe," says I.
   "Takes more than guns to kill a man," says Joe. "I didn't die."
   Says Joe, "I didn't die."

4. And standing there as big as life and smiling with his eyes,
   Joe says, "What they forgot to kill went on to organize,
   Went on to organize."

5. "Joe Hill ain't dead," he says to me. "Joe Hill ain't never died.
   Where working men are out on strike, Joe Hill is at their side.
   Joe Hill is at their side."

6. "From San Diego up to Maine, in every mine and mill,
   Where workers strike and organize," says he, "you'll find Joe Hill."
   Says he, "You'll find Joe Hill."

JOHN HENRY

WEST VIRGINIA

John Henry was said to be a real-life hero, a mighty railroad worker who by 1870
was pounding steel spikes into railroad ties faster than anyone alive. Then, to protest new machines that were replacing human labor, he set himself up in a race
against a steam drill. John Henry won, but burst a blood vessel and died that night,
at age thirty-four. The machine age had arrived. Yet the "steel-driving man" lived
on in dozens of songs and legends, the tales about his strength growing taller over
time.

Clap your hands

1. When John Hen - ry was___ a lit - tle ba - by___ sit - ting on his pa - pa's knee, Well, he picked up a ham-mer and a lit - tle piece of steel, said, "Ham-mer's gon - na be the death of me, Lord, Lord, Ham-mer's gon-na be the death of me, This ham-mer's gon - na be the death of

me,   Lord,   Lord,   Ham-mer's gon-na   be   the death of   me."

2. Well, the Captain said to John Henry,
   "Gonna bring that steam drill round.
   Gonna bring that steam drill out on the job.
   Gonna whup that steel on down, Lord, Lord." (4 times)

3. Well, John Henry said to the Captain,
   "Lord, a man ain't nothing but a man,
   But before I'd let your steam drill beat me down,
   I'd die with a hammer in my hand, Lord, Lord." (4 times)

4. Now the Captain said to John Henry,
   "I believe that mountain's caving in."
   John Henry said right back to the Captain,
   "Ain't nothing but my hammer sucking wind, Lord, Lord." (4 times)

5. Now the Captain said to John Henry,
   "What is that storm I hear?"
   John Henry said, "Captain, that ain't no storm.
   That's just my hammer in the air, Lord, Lord." (4 times)

6. Now the man that invented the steam drill,
   He thought he was mighty fine.
   But John Henry drove fifteen feet,
   The steam drill only made nine, Lord, Lord. (4 times)

7. John Henry hammered in the mountains;
   His hammer was striking fire.
   But he worked so hard, it broke his poor heart,
   And he laid down his hammer and he died, Lord, Lord. (4 times)

8. They took John Henry to the graveyard,
   And they buried him in the sand.
   And ev'ry engine comes a-roaring by
   Whistles, "There lies a steel-driving man, Lord, Lord." (4 times)

9. John Henry had a little baby;
   You could hold him in the palm of your hand;
   And the last words I heard that poor boy say,
   "My daddy was a steel-driving man, Lord, Lord." (4 times)

LITTLE BOXES

Words and music: MALVINA REYNOLDS

Though Malvina Reynolds (1900–1978) didn't actually write a song every day before breakfast, as has been said, she *was* prolific. One day in 1962, on her way to appear in concert near San Francisco, she was suddenly overwhelmed with emotion by the look-alike houses of Daly City. She asked her husband to drive for her, wrote this ironic song on the spot, and performed it that night. In an era when mindless conformity was something to particularly avoid, this song became a popular anthem.

Cheeky

1. Lit - tle box - es on the hill - side, lit - tle box - es made of tick - y tack - y, Lit - tle box - es on the hill - side, lit - tle

box - es all the same. There's a green one and a

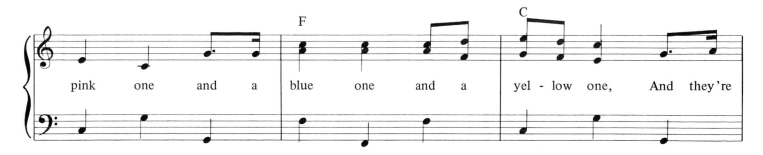

pink one and a blue one and a yel - low one, And they're

all made out of tick - y tack - y and they all look just the same.

2. And the people in the houses all went to the university,
   Where they all were put in boxes, and they came out all the same.
   And there's doctors and there's lawyers and business executives,
   And they're all made out of ticky tacky and they all look just the same.

3. And they all play on the golf course and drink their martinis dry,
   And they all have pretty children and the children go to school.
   And the children go to summer camp and then to the university,
   Where they all get put in boxes and they all come out the same.

MAMA DON'T ALLOW

TRADITIONAL AMERICAN

This old song begs for new verses. Perhaps going back to days when all music was considered the devil's work, Mama traditionally forbids musical fun and partying of any sort. *Your* verses can include anything you've been told not to do in polite company—from hiccuping to nose-picking to name-calling . . .

Ungentlemanly and unladylike

1. Ma - ma don't al - low no gui - tar play - in' round here,

I say that Ma - ma don't al - low no gui - tar play - in' round

here._____ Well, we don't care what

Ma - ma don't al - low. Gon-na play that mu - sic a - ny - how,____

Ma - ma don't al-low no gui - tar play-in' round here.____

2. Mama don't allow no piano playin' round here, etc.

3. Mama don't allow no hand clappin' round here, etc.

4. Mama don't allow no foot stompin' round here, etc.

5. Mama don't allow no singin' round here, etc.
   Gonna sing my head off anyhow, etc.

6. Mama don't allow no loud-mouth talkin' round here, etc.
   Gonna shoot my mouth off anyhow, etc.

7. Mama don't allow no nothin' goin' round here.
   Mama don't allow no nothin' goin' round here.
   Well, I don't see why my Mama won't allow.
   She was once as young as we are now.
   Mama don't allow no nothin' goin' round here.

MICHAEL, ROW THE BOAT ASHORE

This combination sea chantey—black spiritual comes from the Georgia Sea Islands, where over a hundred years ago enslaved blacks worked on plantations. Each plantation had its own boats and a crew of slaves known for its original work songs. Here Michael might have been a boat's lead oarsman, or perhaps the song is about the archangel Michael. Jordan River symbolized freedom, and to runaway slaves, stepping into its chilly waters meant throwing slave owners' dogs off their scent.

Electrically

1. Mi - chael, row the boat a - shore. Al - le - lu - ia! Mi - chael, row the boat a - shore. Al - le - lu - ia!

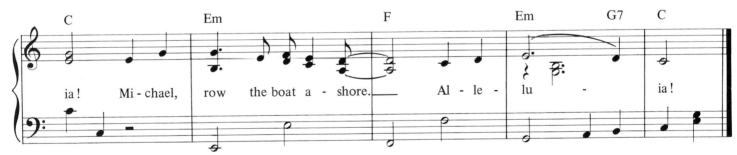

2. Michael's boat is a music boat. Alleluia!
   Michael's boat is a music boat. Alleluia!

3. Sister, help to trim the sail. Alleluia!
   Sister, help to trim the sail. Alleluia!

4. Jordan River is chilly and cold. Alleluia!
   Chills the body but not the soul. Alleluia!

5. The river is deep and the river is wide. Alleluia!
   Milk and honey on the other side. Alleluia!

6. If you get there before I do. Alleluia!
   Tell my people I'm coming too. Alleluia!

THE MOCKINGBIRD SONG
or, Hush, Little Baby

APPALACHIA / ALABAMA

Popular in the South in pioneer days, this descends from an old English nursery rhyme. Now it's possibly the best-known lullaby in America, and whether it's Mama or Papa buying the gifts, it's another good song for making up your own verses.

Drowsy

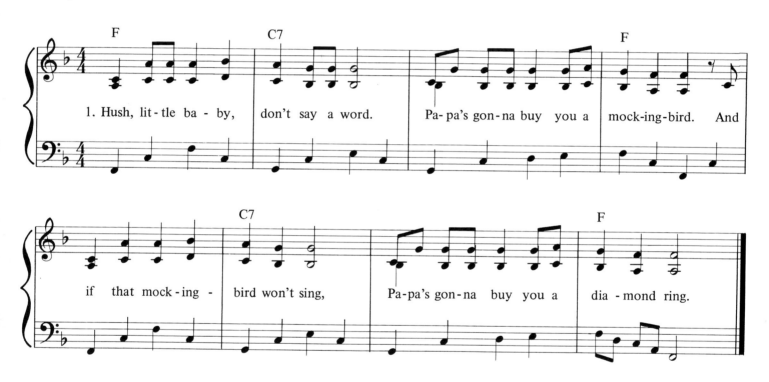

1. Hush, lit-tle ba-by, don't say a word. Pa-pa's gon-na buy you a mock-ing-bird. And if that mock-ing-bird won't sing, Pa-pa's gon-na buy you a dia-mond ring.

2. And if that diamond ring is brass,
   Papa's gonna buy you a looking glass.
   And if that looking glass gets broke,
   Papa's gonna buy you a billy goat.

3. And if that billy goat won't pull,
   Papa's gonna buy you a cart and bull.
   And if that cart and bull turn over,
   Papa's gonna buy you a dog named Rover.

4. And if that dog named Rover won't bark,
   Papa's gonna buy you a horse and cart.
   And if that horse and cart fall down,
   You'll still be the sweetest little baby in town.

74

THE MOTORCYCLE SONG

Words and music: ARLO GUTHRIE

Woody Guthrie bought his son, Arlo, a guitar for his sixth birthday, and by age ten Arlo was performing in public. One of his first protest songs was about a math test, sung to the tune of his father's "So Long, It's Been Good to Know You." The same year that Woody Guthrie died — 1967 — twenty-year-old Arlo reached fame with "Alice's Restaurant," a very funny, very long protest song. Although many of his songs take up social and moral issues, it's hard to find a moral here . . . except maybe that not much rhymes with "motorcycle."

Silly

CHORUS

I don't want a pick-le,

Just want to ride on my mo - tor-sick - le.   And

I don't want a tick - le,   'Cause

I'd rath - er ride__ on my mo - tor-sick - le.

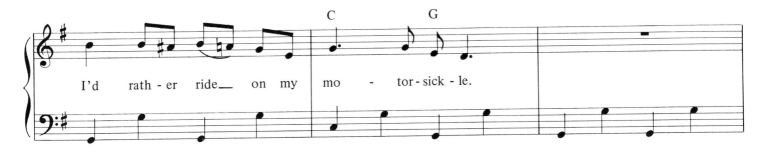

And   I   don't want   to   die,

Just want to ride__ on my mo - tor -

cy - cle.

VERSE

It was late last night the oth - er day,

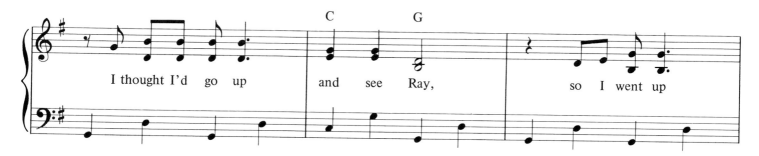

I thought I'd go up and see Ray, so I went up

and I saw Ray,— There was on-ly one thing Ray could say was:

FINE

D.C. al Fine

OH, SUSANNA!

Customers at the Eagle Ice Cream Parlor in Pittsburgh were the first audience for
this nonsense song. It was 1847, and Stephen Foster (1826–1864) was only twenty-
one. Two years later the "forty-niners" of the California gold rush took up the
bouncy rhythm and made this the most popular song in America. Foster never
made much money from "Oh, Susanna!" Still, he wrote later, "The two fifty-dollar
bills I received had the effect of starting me on my present vocation as a song-writer."
Foster created some two hundred more songs, including "Beautiful Dreamer,"
"Swanee River," "Jeanie with the Light Brown Hair," and "Camptown Races."

Spunky

me, For I come from A - la - ba - ma with a ban - jo on my knee.

2. I had a dream the other night, when everything was still;
I thought I saw Susanna come a-walking down the hill.
A red, red rose was in her cheek, a tear was in her eye;
I said to her, "Susanna, girl, Susanna, don't you cry."

CHORUS

OLD JOE CLARK

SOUTHERN

Some say Joe Clark was a moonshiner in the Virginia hills, a veteran of the War of 1812, or a popular banjo player from Clay County, Kentucky. Still, the hundreds of verses to this classic square-dance tune have more to do with what words will fit to its irresistible rhythm than with any one person.

Kick up your heels

1. I used to live on the moun-tain-top; Now I live in town, I'm

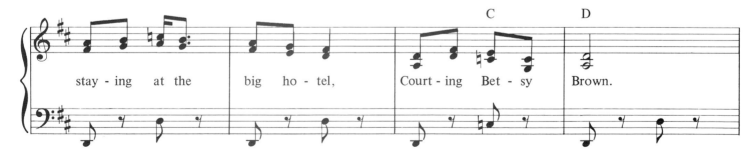

stay-ing at the big ho-tel, Court-ing Bet-sy Brown.

CHORUS

Fare you well, Old Joe Clark, fare you well, I'm bound.

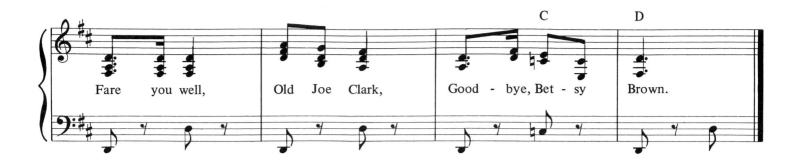

Fare you well, Old Joe Clark, Good - bye, Bet - sy Brown.

2. Old Joe Clark, he had a house
   Sixteen stories high.
   And every story in that house
   Was full of chicken pie.
   CHORUS

3. Old Joe Clark, he had a mule,
   His name was Morgan Brown.
   And every tooth in that mule's head
   Was sixteen inches around.
   CHORUS

4. Old Joe had a chicken coop
   Eighteen stories high.
   And every chicken in that coop
   Turned into chicken pie.
   CHORUS

5. When I was a little girl,
   I used to play with toys.
   But now I am a bigger girl,
   I'd rather play with boys.
   CHORUS

6. When I was a little boy,
   I used to want a knife.
   But now I am a bigger boy,
   All I want is a wife.
   CHORUS

ON TOP OF OLD SMOKY

Sometimes in the Blue Ridge Mountains the fog gets so thick that the mountains seem made of smoke. No one knows who wrote this ballad about "Old Smoky," but its wistful admission of loneliness made it popular in pioneer days, even more popular in a 1951 million-selling record by the Weavers, and a familiar 1960s folk-song standard. Ultimately it's lent itself to many parodies, including "On Top of Spaghetti" and "I Shot My Poor Teacher."

Try to be serious

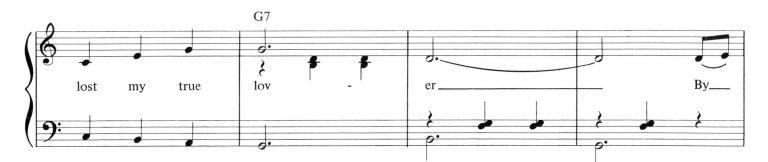

court - ing so slow.

2. Well, courting's a pleasure
   And parting is grief,
   But a false-hearted lover
   Is worse than a thief.

3. A thief, he will rob you
   And take all you have,
   But a false-hearted lover
   Will send you to your grave.

4. They'll hug you and kiss you
   And tell you more lies
   Than the cross ties on the railroad
   Or the stars in the skies.

5. They'll tell you they love you
   Just to give your heart ease,
   And just as soon as your back's turned,
   They'll court whom they please.

6. I'll go back to Old Smoky,
   Old Smoky so high,
   Where the wild birds and turtledoves
   Can hear my sad cry.

RED RIVER VALLEY

The Red River flows from Texas to join the Mississippi in Louisiana, but this ballad originally had nothing to do with it. Instead the song began in New York State as "In the Bright Mohawk Valley" and traveled west, reaching its lasting fame as a favorite cowboy love song. Its mournful message has led people to request that it be played at funerals, and it's had two movies named after it, one starring Gene Autry and the other, Roy Rogers.

Not too sentimental

1. From this val - ley they say you are go - ing;

We will miss your bright eyes and sweet smile,

For they say you are tak - ing the sun - shine

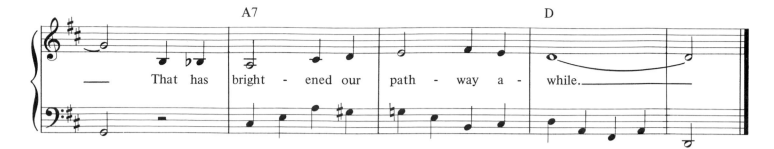

That has bright - ened our path - way a - while._____

2. Come and sit by my side if you love me.
   Do not hasten to bid me adieu,
   But remember the Red River Valley
   And the cowboy that loves [girl that has loved] you so true.

3. Won't you think of this valley you're leaving?
   Oh, how lonely, how sad it will be.
   Oh, think of the fond heart you're breaking
   And the grief you are causing me.

THE RIDDLE SONG
◖ or, I Gave My Love a Cherry

KENTUCKY

This love song made up of riddles can be traced back almost six hundred years, to rural Britain and an old ballad called "Captain Walker's Courtship." By the mid-1700s Kentucky mountaineers following Daniel Boone westward had made it their own. Further westward migration . . . and almost every American child has heard this song, especially since its revival after World War II.

Like an opera singer

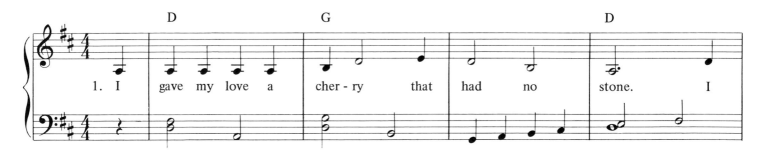

1. I gave my love a cher-ry that had no stone. I

gave my love a chick-en that had no bone. I

told my love a sto - ry that had no end. I

gave my love a ba - by with no cry - ing.

2. How can there be a cherry that has no stone?
   How can there be a chicken that has no bone?
   How can there be a story that has no end?
   How can there be a baby with no crying?

3. A cherry, when it's blooming, it has no stone.
   A chicken, when it's pipping, it has no bone.
   The story that I love you, it has no end.
   A baby, when it's sleeping, has no crying.

ROCK ISLAND LINE

SOUTHERN

Traditionally this is known as yet another classic train song. But lumberjacks have sung it as well, the title and lyrics changing to fit the locale of the work camp. The first recording of this version, about the Chicago, Rock Island & Pacific Railroad, was made by Kelley Pace and other convicts at the Cumins State Prison Farm in Arkansas. The song is most frequently associated with Leadbelly, who first recorded it in 1934.

Full tilt

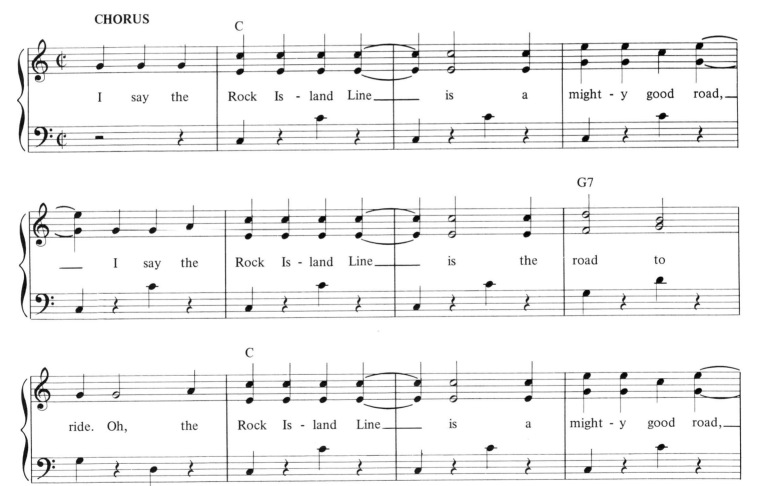

CHORUS

I say the Rock Is - land Line____ is a might - y good road, ____ I say the Rock Is - land Line____ is the road to ride. Oh, the Rock Is - land Line____ is a might - y good road, ____

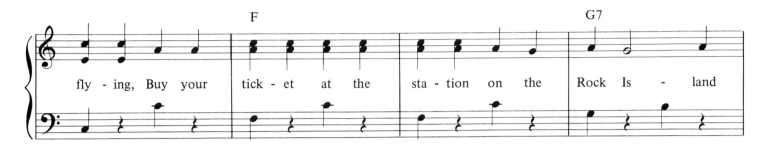

If you want to ride it, got to ride it like you're fly - ing, Buy your tick - et at the sta - tion on the Rock Is - land Line.

1. I may be right and I may be wrong, I know you're gon - na miss me when I'm____ gone.

2. A-B-C, double X-Y-Z.
   Cat's in the cupboard, but he can't see me.

3. Jesus died to save our sins.
   Glory be to God, we're gonna need him again.

SHALL WE GATHER AT THE RIVER?

BROOKLYN, NEW YORK

Nineteenth-century revivalist meetings often featured this hymn by Robert Lowry, the musically inclined pastor of the Hanson Place Baptist Church in Brooklyn, New York. His collection of hymns, *Bright Jewels*, sold over a million copies. In 1864 he wrote this, surely his most durable song, about the pleasures of heavenly peace.

Stand up straight

1. Shall we gath - er at the riv - er, Where bright an - gel feet have trod,_____ With its crys - tal tide for - ev - er Flow - ing by the___ throne of___ God?

CHORUS

Yes, we'll gath - er at the riv - er, the beau - ti - ful, the beau - ti - ful___ riv - er,

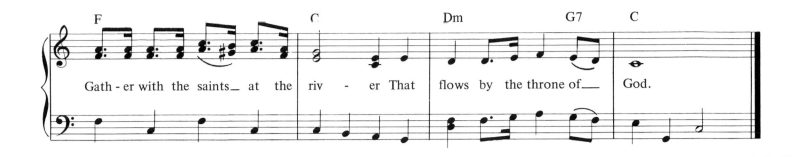

Gather with the saints at the river That flows by the throne of God.

2. Ere we reach the shining river,
   Lay we every burden down.
   Grace our spirits will deliver
   And provide a robe and crown.
   CHORUS

3. Soon we'll reach the silver river.
   Soon our pilgrimage will cease.
   Soon our happy hearts will quiver
   With the melody of peace.
   CHORUS

SHE'LL BE COMING ROUND THE MOUNTAIN

In the 1890s Midwestern railroad gangs took a spiritual, "When the Chariot Comes," and made this joyful work song out of it. Locomotives frequently were personalized into "he" or "she," "six white horses" might refer to the engine's horsepower, and the sight and sounds of a train coming around the bend were always thrilling. Trains brought supplies, a break in the daily routine, mail from loved ones. Depending on the terrain, a train might be seen coming for half a day— a good long time to be singing!

With a driving rhythm

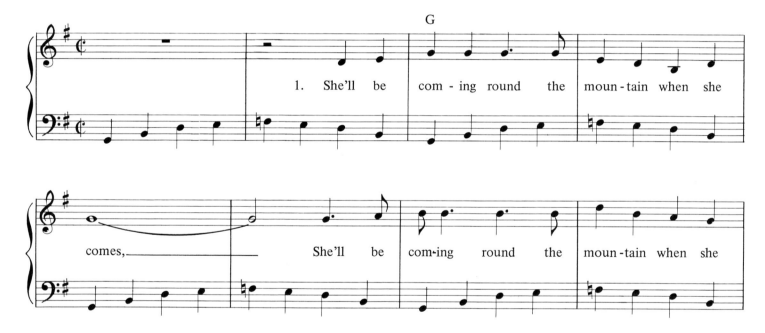

1. She'll be com-ing round the moun-tain when she comes,____ She'll be com-ing round the moun-tain when she comes.____

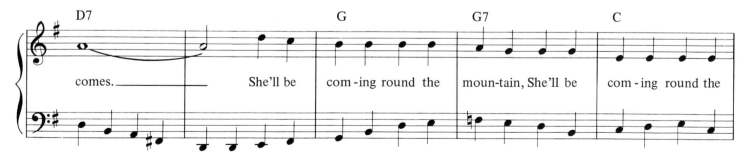

She'll be com-ing round the moun-tain, She'll be com-ing round the

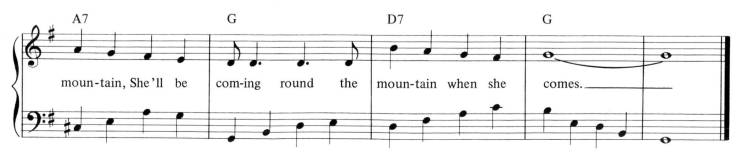

moun-tain, She'll be com-ing round the moun-tain when she comes.____

2. She'll be driving six white horses when she comes, etc.

3. Oh, we'll all go down to meet her when she comes, etc.

4. Oh, we'll kill the old red rooster when she comes, etc.

5. We'll be singing "Alleluia" when she comes, etc.

6. She'll be wearing pink pajamas when she comes, etc.

Make up your own verses!

SHENANDOAH

MISSOURI

Shenandoah, an Algonquian word meaning "daughter of the stars," is a river in Virginia, but it is both a person *and* a river in this sea chantey. In the early nineteenth century the song was solely about a trader in the Missouri River area who fell in love with the daughter of the Algonquian chief Shenandoah. American sailors heading down the Mississippi River took up the slow, rolling melody for the slow, rolling work of hoisting a ship's anchor, changing words to suit their purpose.

Passionate

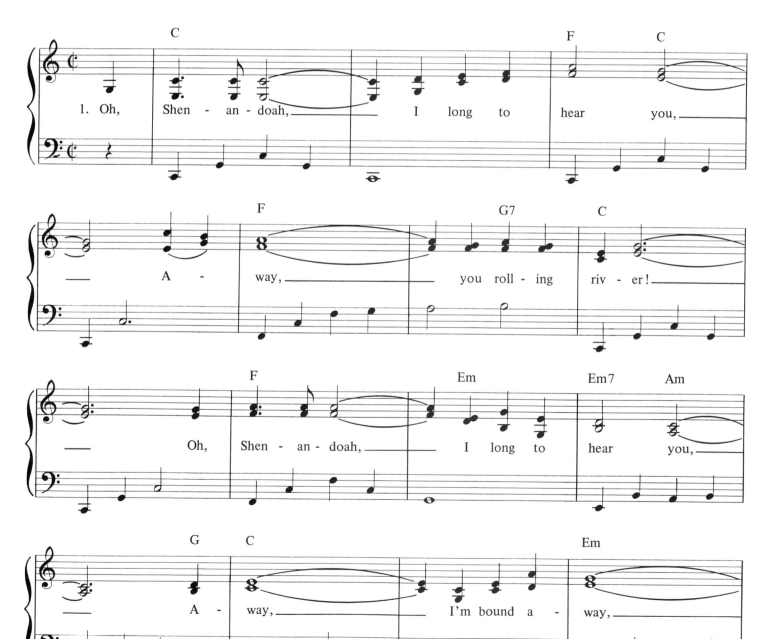

'Cross the wide Mis - sou - ri!

2. Oh, Shenandoah, I love your daughter.
   Away, you rolling river!
   For her I'd cross the rolling water.
   Away, I'm bound away, 'cross the wide Missouri.

3. Oh, Shenandoah, I'm bound to leave you.
   Away, you rolling river!
   Oh, Shenandoah, I'll not deceive you.
   Away, I'm bound away, 'cross the wide Missouri.

SHILOH, LIZA JANE
ℂ or, Scraping Up Sand in the Bottom of the Sea

MISSOURI

This nonsense song was used as play-party entertainment in Missouri during a time when the only dancing allowed was movement during a singing game. Is the first verse about a whale, a machine that dredges sand from the ocean, a dog digging a hole, or someone planting a garden? Feel free to use your imagination to imitate the motions described in each verse.

Frisky

1. Scrap-ing up sand in the bot-tom of the sea, Shi - loh, Shi - loh.
Scrap-ing up sand in the bot-tom of the sea, Shi - loh, Li - za Jane.

CHORUS

Oh, how I love her, Oh, Li - za Jane,

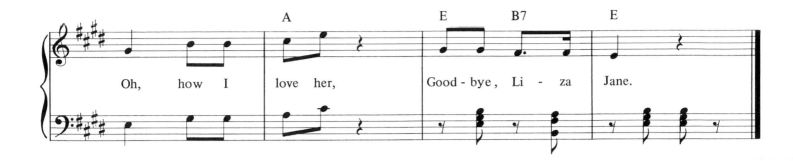

Oh, how I love her, Good-bye, Li - za Jane.

2. Black those boots and make them shine, etc.

CHORUS

3. A hump-back mule I'm bound to ride, etc.

CHORUS

4. Hopped up a chicken and he flew upstairs, etc.

CHORUS

THE SLOOP *JOHN B.*

NEW ENGLAND

The melody for this hundred-year-old song is believed to come from New England. But the words refer to a young sailor's disagreeable journey around Nassau—in the Bahamas off the coast of Florida—and its offbeat rhythm gives it a calypso feeling. It has become popular all over America and a particular hit for the Beach Boys.

As if you're seasick

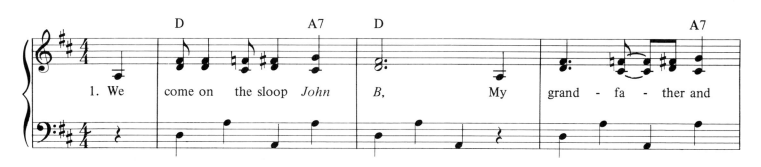

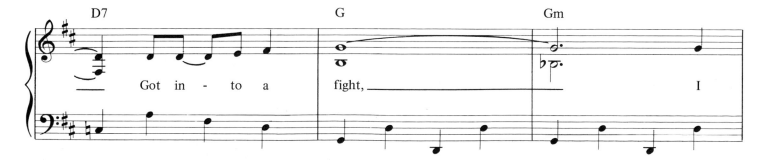

feel so break up, I want to go home.

CHORUS.   So hoist up the *John B.* sails.
See how the mainsail sets.
Send for the captain ashore, let me go home.
Let me go home, let me go home.
I feel so break up, I want to go home.

2. The first mate, oh, he got drunk,
   Broke up the people's trunk.
   Constable had to come and take him away.
   Sheriff Johnstone, please leave me alone.
   I feel so break up, I want to go home.
                                        CHORUS

3. The poor cook, oh, he got fits,
   Throw away all of the grits.
   Then he took and eat up all of my corn.
   Let me go home, I want to go home.
   This is the worst trip I've ever been on.
                                        CHORUS

SO LONG, IT'S BEEN GOOD TO KNOW YOU
ℭ or, Dusty Old Dust

Words and music: WOODY GUTHRIE

Borrowing a melody from "The Ballad of Billy the Kid," Woody Guthrie (1912–1967) wrote this somewhat bitter song in 1935 to commemorate the deadly dust storms that forced him to leave his native Oklahoma for California. There he joined half a million other homeless, desperately poor "Okies." Guthrie went on to become a major influence on several generations of folksingers, writing more than a thousand songs, many of which seem likely to live forever.

Gently

1. I've sung this song, but I'll sing it___ a - gain, of the

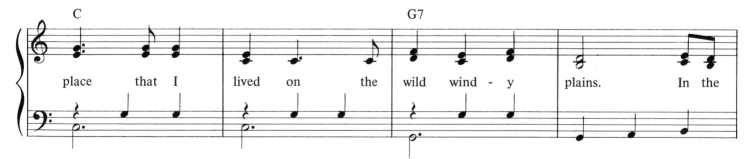

place that I lived on the wild wind - y plains. In the

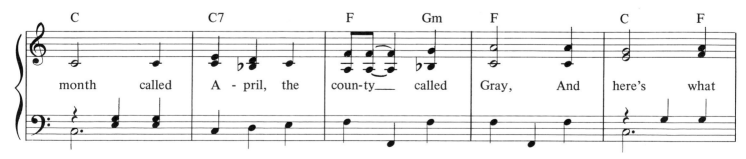

month called A - pril, the coun-ty___ called Gray, And here's what

CHORUS

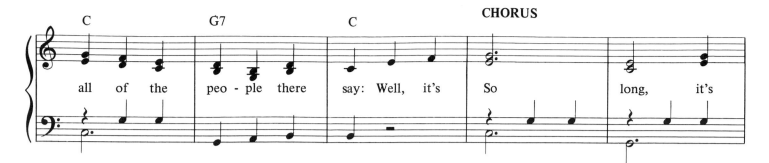

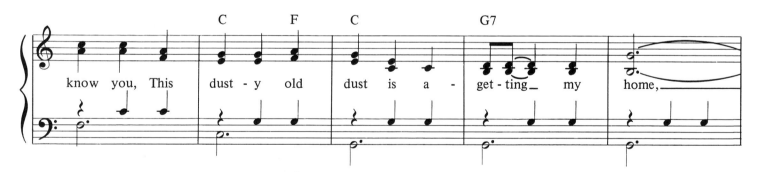

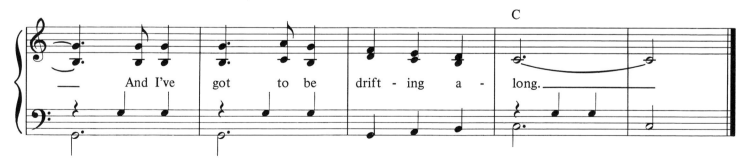

2. Well, the dust storm, it hit, and it hit like thunder.
   It dusted us over, it dusted us under.
   It blocked out the traffic, it blocked out the sun,
   And straight for home all the people did run, saying,
   CHORUS

3. Well, the sweethearts, they sat in the dark and they sparked,
   They hugged and kissed in that dusty old dark.
   They sighed and cried, hugged and kissed,
   But instead of marriage they were talking like this: Honey,
   CHORUS

4. The telephone rang and it jumped off the wall,
   And that was the preacher a making his call.
   He said, "Kind friend, this might be the end.
   You got your last chance at salvation from sin."
   CHORUS

5. The churches were jammed, the churches were packed,
   And that dusty old dust storm it blowed so black
   That the preacher could not read a word of his text,
   And he folded his specs and he took up collection, said,
   CHORUS

STEWBALL

An Irish ballad about "Sku-ball" first appeared in print in England in 1822. In an important horse race, that year's prize thoroughbred mare, Miss Portly, was matched against Sku-ball, an ordinary horse with no pedigree. The name of the winning horse was one of many changes made as this ballad evolved into a Southern work song—especially popular in Kentucky, home of the most famous horse race in America—the Kentucky Derby.

Heroic

1. Oh, Stew-ball was a good horse, And he held a high head, And the mane on his fore-top Was as fine as silk thread.

2. I rode him in England,
   I rode him in Spain.
   He was never a loser,
   And I always did gain.

3. So come all you gamblers
   From near and from far.
   Don't bet your gold dollar
   On that little gray mare.

4. Most likely she'll stumble;
   Most likely she'll fall.
   But you never will lose
   On my noble Stewball.

5. As they were a-riding
   'Bout halfway around,
   That gray mare she stumbled
   And fell to the ground.

6. And away out yonder,
   Ahead of them all,
   Came prancing and dancing
   My noble Stewball.

SWEET BETSY FROM PIKE

CALIFORNIA

Sweet Betsy was the best example of the special kind of woman who moved to California during the gold-rush days: fearless, independent, and ready to party. She arrived by covered wagon in the mining town of Placerville, having made the 2,000-mile trek from Pike County, Missouri. This celebration of the legendary Betsy, first published in 1858, descends from a seventeenth-century British ballad called "Willkins and Dinah."

Gutsy

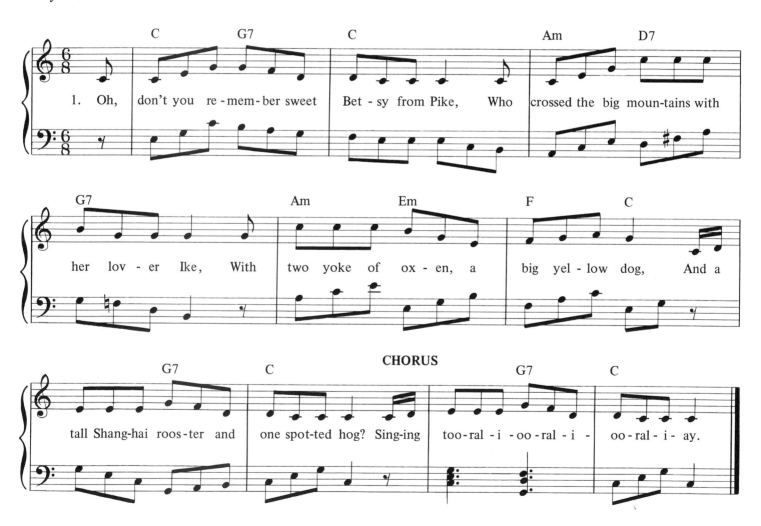

2. One evening quite early they camped on the Platte.
'Twas near by the road on a green shady flat,
Where Betsy, quite tired, she laid down to repose,
While with wonder Ike gazed on his Pike County rose.
CHORUS

3. They soon reached the desert, where Betsy gave out,
And down in the sand she lay rolling about,
While Ike, in great tears, he looked on in surprise,
Saying, "Betsy, get up, you'll get sand in your eyes."
CHORUS

4. Sweet Betsy got up in a great deal of pain
   And declared she'd go back to Pike County again.
   Then Ike heaved a sigh and they fondly embraced,
   And she traveled along with his arm round her waist.
   CHORUS

5. The Shanghai ran off and the cattle all died.
   The last piece of bacon that morning was fried.
   Poor Ike got discouraged, and Betsy got mad.
   The dog wagged his tail and looked wonderfully sad.
   CHORUS

6. One morning they climbed up a very high hill
   And with wonder looked down into old Placerville.
   Ike shouted and said, as he cast his eyes down,
   "Sweet Betsy, my darling, we've got to Hangtown."
   CHORUS

7. Long Ike and sweet Betsy attended a dance,
   Where Ike wore a pair of his Pike County pants.
   Sweet Betsy was covered with ribbons and rings.
   Quoth Ike, "You're an angel, but where are your wings?"
   CHORUS

8. Long Ike and sweet Betsy got married, of course,
   But Ike, getting jealous, obtained a divorce.
   And Betsy, well satisfied, said with a smile,
   "There are six good men waiting within half a mile."
   CHORUS

TAKE ME OUT TO THE BALL GAME

AMERICAN BASEBALL PARKS

Baseball fans have yelled and cheered this anthem to the American national sport since 1908, when it was first published. Jack Norworth, a vaudeville actor, wrote the words. Albert von Tilzer, part of a musical family from Indianapolis, wrote the music—some twenty years before he actually saw his first baseball game.

Sunny

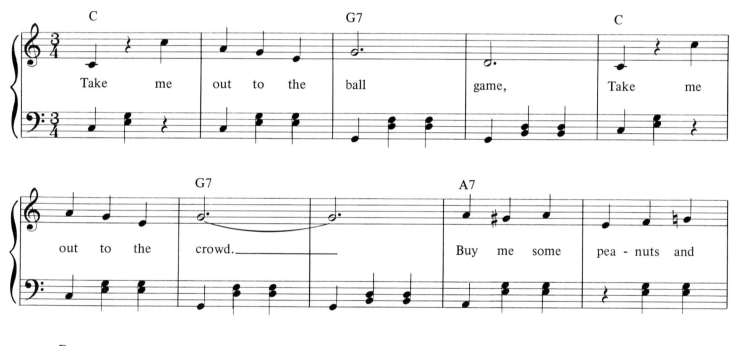

Take me out to the ball game, Take me out to the crowd.____ Buy me some pea-nuts and

Crack - er Jack, I don't care if I nev - er come

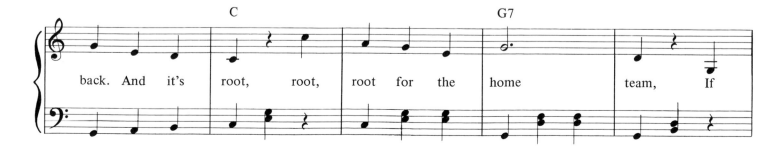

back. And it's root, root, root for the home team, If

they don't win it's a shame._____ For it's one,

two, three strikes, "You're out!" at the old ball game.

TELL ME WHY

TRADITIONAL AMERICAN

This old camp favorite makes a sweet love song—from parent to child and back again, or between friends . . . or from Garrison Keillor, host of *A Prairie Home Companion,* to his audience, in what became one of the radio show's theme songs.

In a voice like honey

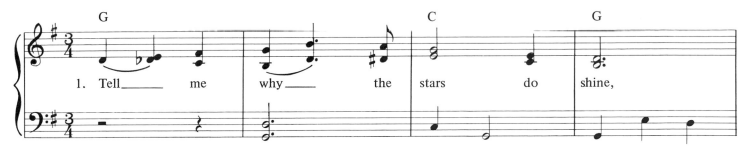

1. Tell___ me why___ the stars do shine,

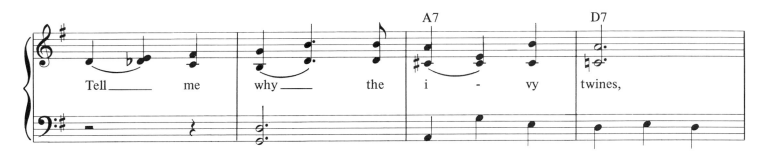

Tell___ me why___ the i - vy twines,

Tell___ me why___ the sky's so blue,

And I will tell you just why I love you.

2. Because God made the stars to shine,
   Because God made the ivy twine,
   Because God made the sky so blue,
   Because God made you, that's why I love you.

113

THERE'S A HOLE IN THE BUCKET

PENNSYLVANIA

This duet comes from the Pennsylvania Dutch, descendants of the earliest German settlers of the lush valleys in southeastern Pennsylvania. Traditionally boys sing the part of literal-minded, patient Henry, while girls sing the part of know-it-all Liza, but it can be fun to reverse the roles too.

Saucy

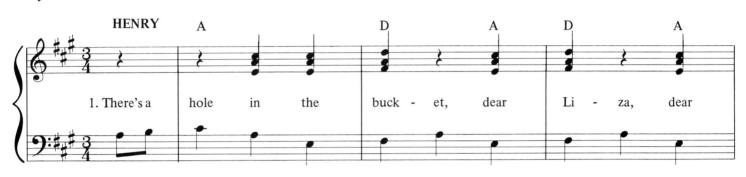

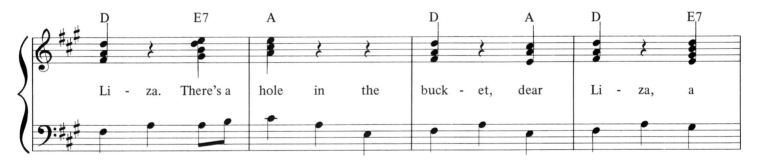

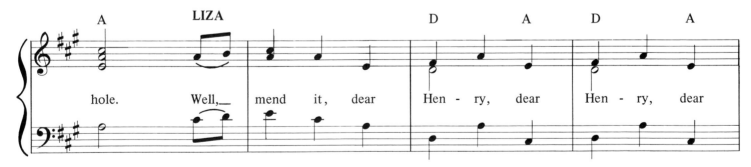

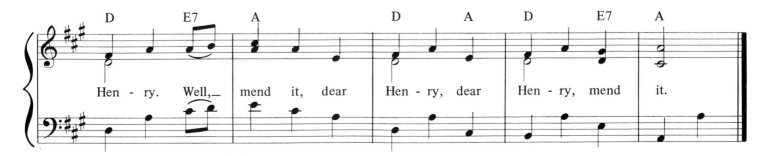

2. *Henry.* With what shall I mend it? etc.
   Liza. With a straw, etc.

3. *Henry.* But the straw is too long, etc.
   Liza. Well, then cut it, etc.

4. *Henry.* With what shall I cut it? etc.
   Liza. With an ax, etc.

5. *Henry.* But the ax is too dull, etc.
   Liza. Well, then sharpen it, etc.

6. *Henry.* With what shall I sharpen it? etc.
   Liza. With a stone, etc.

7. *Henry.* But the stone is too dry, etc.
   Liza. Then wet it, etc.

8. *Henry.* With what shall I wet it? etc.
   Liza. With water, etc.

9. *Henry.* In what shall I carry it? etc.
   Liza. In a bucket, etc.

10. *Henry.* But there's a hole in the bucket, etc.
    Liza. Then mend it, oh, Henry!

THIS LAND IS YOUR LAND

Words and music: WOODY GUTHRIE

One night in 1940 Woody Guthrie sat in his New York hotel room and wrote a parody of a popular song that bothered him: Irving Berlin's "God Bless America." He used the melody from an old Baptist hymn and ended each verse with "God blessed America for me." By 1944, when Guthrie began performing it, he'd changed this last line to "This land was made for you and me." This version stuck, as Woody Guthrie's "love song to America," and it's become an honorary national anthem.

Proudly

CHORUS

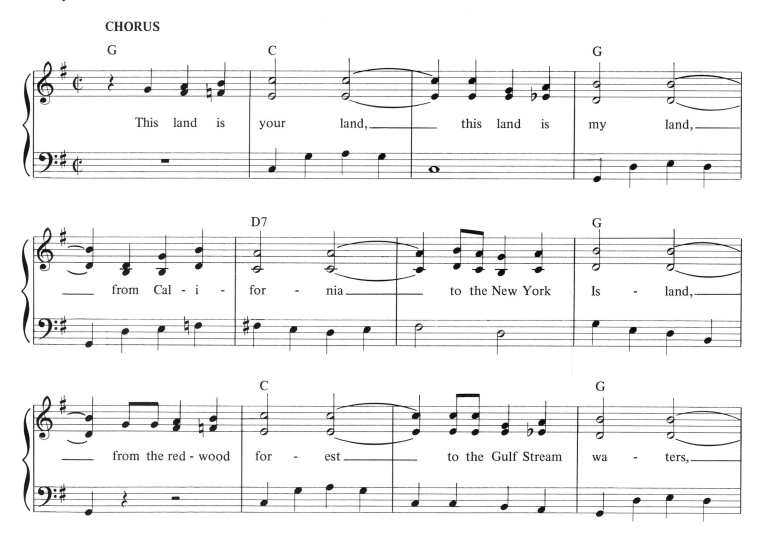

This land is your land, this land is my land, ___ from Cali - for - nia ___ to the New York Is - land, ___ from the red-wood for - est ___ to the Gulf Stream wa - ters,

This land was made for you and me.

1. As I went walking that ribbon of highway,
   I saw above me that endless skyway,
   I saw below me that golden valley—
   This land was made for you and me.
   CHORUS

2. I roamed and rambled, and I followed my footsteps
   To the sparkling sands of her diamond deserts.
   All around me a voice was sounding,
   This land was made for you and me.
   CHORUS

3. When the sun come shining, then I was strolling,
   And the wheat fields waving, and the dust clouds rolling.
   A voice was chanting as the fog was lifting,
   This land was made for you and me.
   CHORUS

4. In the squares of the cities, by the shadow of the steeples,
   In the relief office, I saw my people,
   And some were stumbling and some were wondering if
   This land was made for you and me.
   CHORUS

5. As I went rambling that dusty highway,
   I saw a sign that said, "Private Property,"
   But on the other side it didn't say nothing—
   That side was made for you and me.
   CHORUS

6. Nobody living can ever stop me
   As I go walking my freedom highway.
   Nobody living can make me turn back—
   This land was made for you and me.
   CHORUS

THIS LITTLE LIGHT OF MINE

SOUTHERN

The "little light" in this traditional gospel song can mean many things: love, your own talents and personality, spiritual power, freedom, the ability to make changes. In the 1960s new words relating to black-voter-registration drives and student protests were sung to this old melody.

Fearlessly, with a strong beat

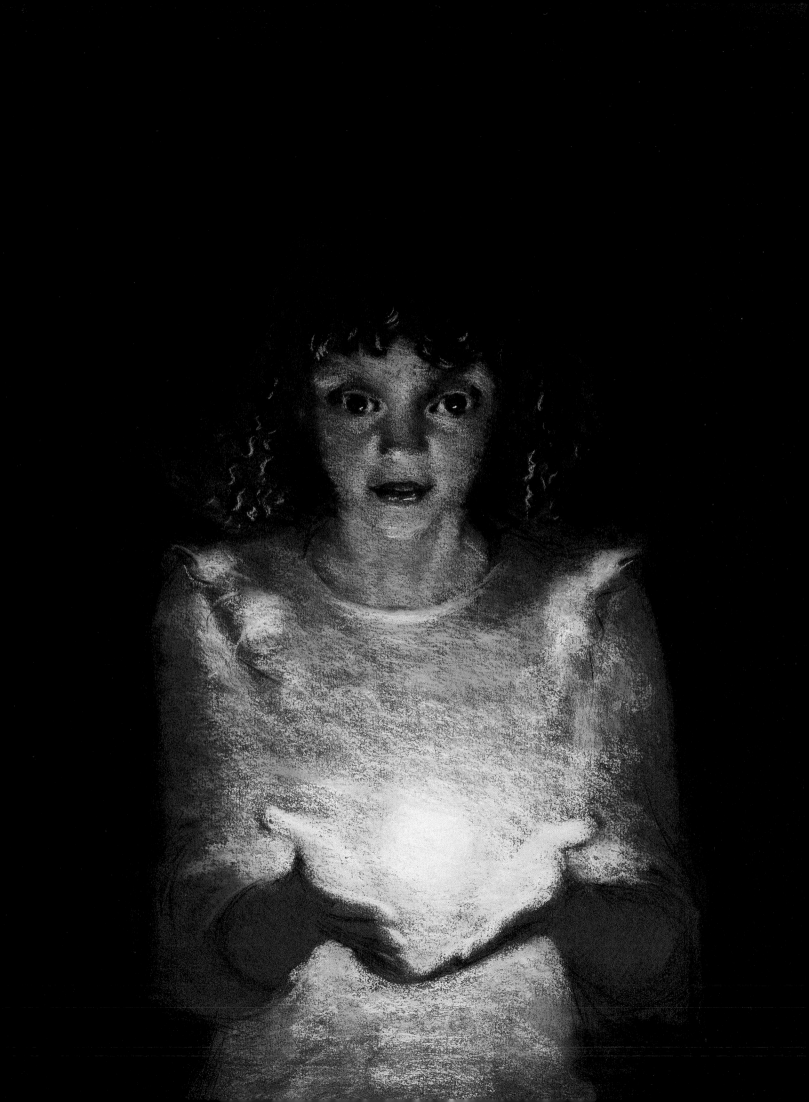

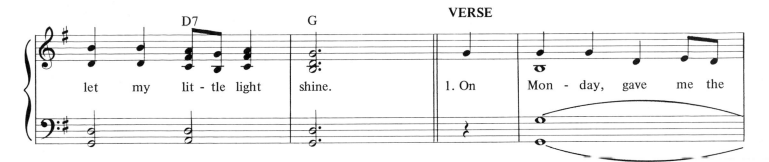

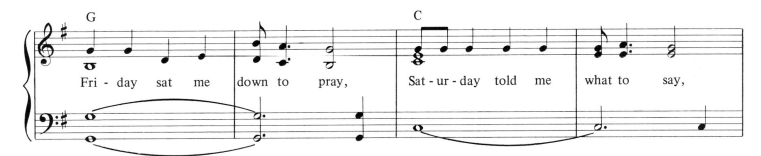

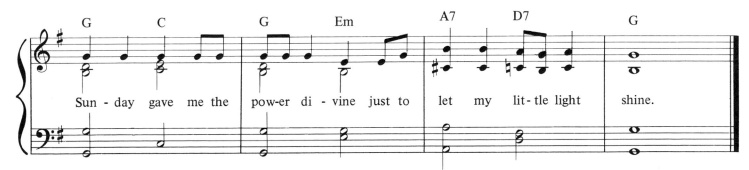

2. The light that shines is the light of love,
   Lights the darkness from above.
   It shines on me and it shines on you,
   Shows what the power of love can do.
   I'm gonna shine my light both far and near.
   I'm gonna shine my light both bright and clear.
   Where there's a dark corner in this land,
   I'm gonna let my little light shine.

'TIS A GIFT TO BE SIMPLE

NEW YORK STATE

Ann Lee, thirty-two years old, founded a new religion in 1767: the United Society of Believers in Christ's Second Appearing. Members were called Shakers because of their dancing during religious services, or sometimes Shaking Quakers because of their religion's similarity to the Quakers'. At their peak the Shakers lived in communities in nine Midwest and Eastern states. The contemporary hymn "Lord of the Dance" uses the melody of this Shaker hymn, first published in 1848. Aaron Copland also used the melody in his ballet *Appalachian Spring*.

Sweetly

'Tis a gift to be sim-ple, 'tis a gift to be free, 'Tis a gift to come down to

where we ought to be. And when we find our-selves in the place just right, 'Twill

be in the val-ley of __ love and de-light. When true sim- plic-i-ty is gained, To

bow and to bend we__ won't be a-shamed. To

be our de-light, till by turn-ing and turn-ing we__ come a-round right.

TURKEY IN THE STRAW

MIDWESTERN

This song is as American a symbol as the Thanksgiving turkey. First sung in New York City in 1834, it's most often associated with rural Midwestern square dances. Every country fiddler knows the classic tune—possibly descended from an old Irish ballad or Southern black song—with its perky rhythm just right for dancing. Over the years it has had endless verses and has been the source of endless parodies.

Dance while you sing

1. As I was a-go-ing on down the road With a ti-red team and a heav-y load, I cracked my whip and the lead-er sprung; I says, "Day - day" to the wa-gon tongue.

CHORUS

Tur-key in the straw, haw, haw, haw. Tur-key in the hay, hay, hay, hay. Roll 'em up and twist 'em up a

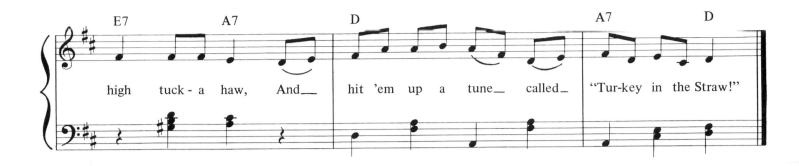

high tuck-a haw, And__ hit 'em up a tune__ called__ "Tur-key in the Straw!"

2. Oh, I went out to milk and I didn't know how.
   I milked the goat instead of the cow.
   A monkey sitting on a pile of straw
   A-winking his eye at his mother-in-law.
                                    CHORUS

3. Well, I met Mr. Catfish coming down the stream.
   Says Mr. Catfish, "What do you mean?"
   I caught Mr. Catfish by the snout
   And turned Mr. Catfish wrong-side out.
                                    CHORUS

4. Came to the river and I couldn't get across,
   So I paid five dollars for an old blind horse.
   Well, he wouldn't go ahead and he wouldn't stand still,
   So he went up and down like an old sawmill.
                                    CHORUS

TURN, TURN, TURN
◖ or, To Everything There Is a Season

Music: Pete Seeger / Words: Ecclesiastes 3:1–8

For months Pete Seeger carried these favorite Bible verses in his pocket before getting a burst of inspiration in 1962 and writing a melody to go with slightly adapted words. Groups such as the Byrds recorded this and further publicized the message that there is a time and place for everything, especially peace. The music and life of Pete Seeger, an enduring presence in American folk music and one of the most influential banjo players ever, frequently involves social causes.

Smoothly

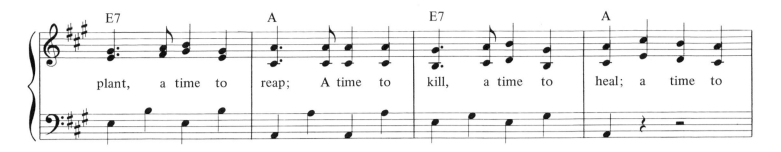

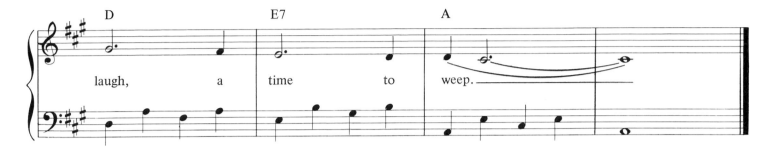

CHORUS

2. A time to build up, a time to break down;
   A time to dance, a time to mourn;
   A time to cast away stones, a time to gather
                        stones together.

CHORUS

3. A time of war, a time of peace;
   A time of love, a time of hate;
   A time you may embrace, a time to refrain
                        from embracing.

CHORUS

4. A time to gain, a time to lose;
   A time to rend, a time to sew;
   A time of love, a time of hate;
   A time of peace, I swear it's not too late.

WE SHALL OVERCOME

SOUTHERN

Before there was "We Are the World" or "Give Peace a Chance," there was this most famous of songs about peace and justice. Written as a Baptist hymn in 1901 and called "I'll Be All Right" or "I'll Overcome Someday," this anthem has undergone many changes; by 1946 black tobacco workers in Charleston, South Carolina, had given it a symbolic meaning—it was about overcoming racism. By the 1960s, civil-rights meetings and nonviolent demonstrations were closing with this song as people linked hands, swayed to the music, and improvised verses. The most recent use of "We Shall Overcome" for inspiration has been by Chinese demonstrators for democracy in 1989.

With dignity

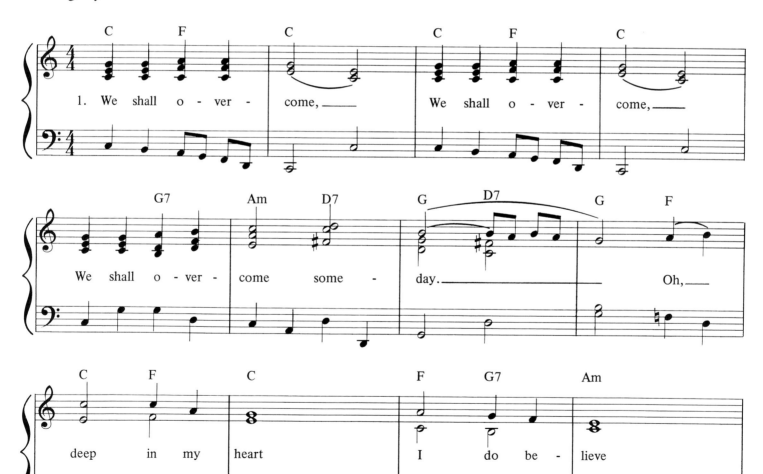

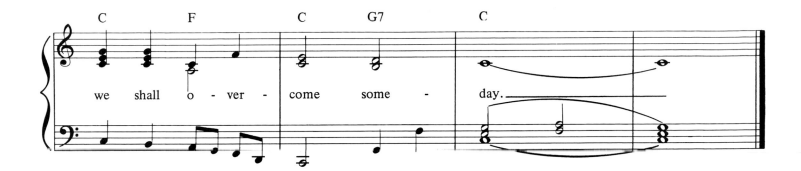

we shall o - ver - come some - day.

2. We'll walk hand in hand, etc.

3. We shall live in peace, etc.

4. We shall all be free, etc.

5. We are not alone, etc.

6. We shall build a new world, etc.

7. We are not afraid, etc.

WHAT HAVE THEY DONE TO THE RAIN?

Words and music: MALVINA REYNOLDS

This song was originally written to protest the effects on ordinary rain of the radio-active fallout from atomic-bomb explosions. But it can be taken as a cry of outrage against the environmental effects of pollution in general. Joan Baez calls it "the gentlest protest song I know."

Plaintively

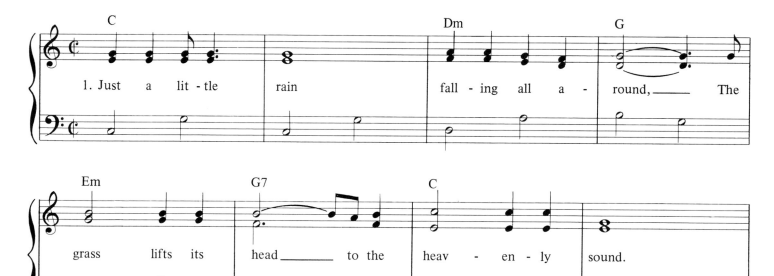

1. Just a lit-tle rain falling all a-round,____ The grass lifts its head____ to the heav-en-ly sound.

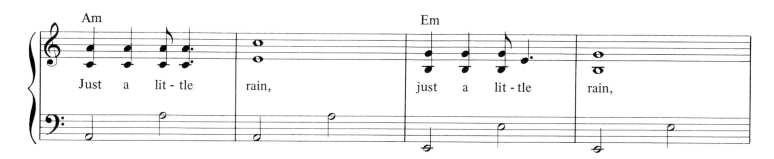

Just a lit-tle rain, just a lit-tle rain,

What have they done____ to the rain?____

CHORUS

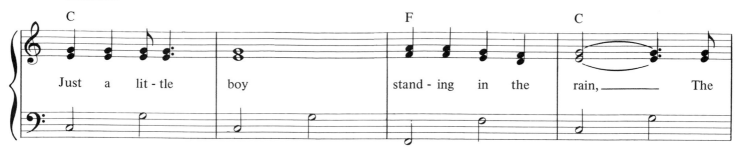

Just a lit-tle boy standing in the rain,_____ The

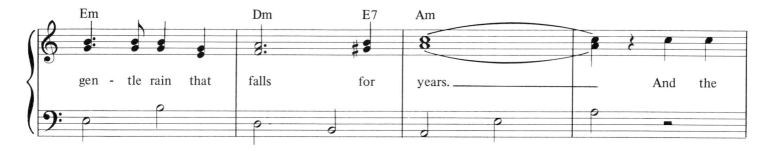

gen-tle rain that falls for years._____ And the

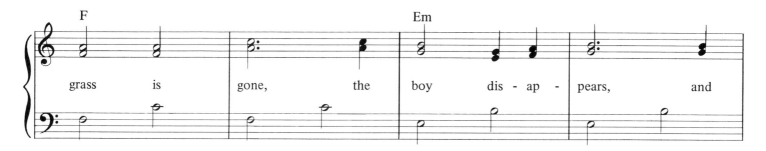

grass is gone, the boy dis-ap - pears, and

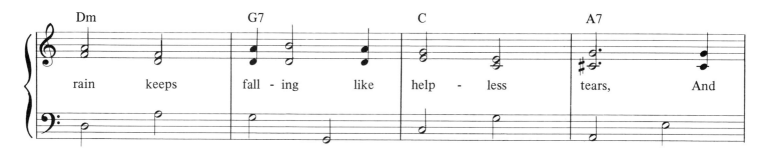

rain keeps fall - ing like help - less tears, And

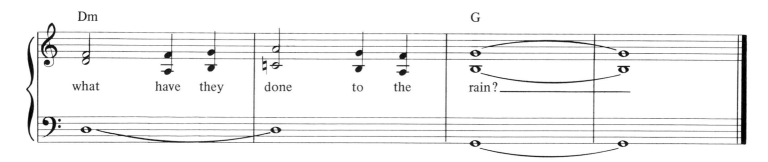

what have they done to the rain?_____

2. Just a little breeze out of the sky,
   The leaves pat their hands as the breeze blows by.
   Just a little breeze with some smoke in its eye,
   What have they done to the rain?

   CHORUS

WILL THE CIRCLE BE UNBROKEN

SOUTHERN

Popular in the South for years, this sacred song has been recorded many times and made into an American favorite. Though literally about a funeral procession, the "circle" can mean many things—the family circle, the cycle of life and death, a person's spirit or soul.

Fervently

1. I was stand - ing   by the   win - dow   on one   cold and cloud - y

day,_____   And I   saw   the   hearse come   roll - ing   for to

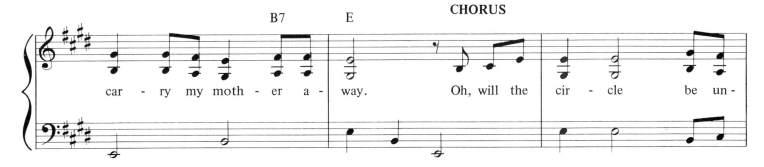

car - ry my moth - er a - way.   Oh, will the   cir - cle   be un-

CHORUS

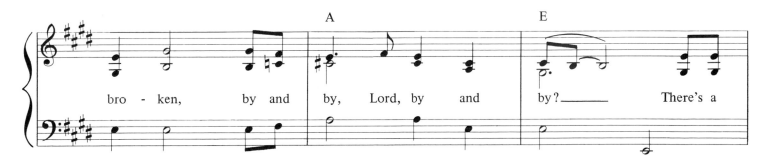

bro - ken,   by and   by,   Lord, by   and   by?_____   There's a

133

bet - ter　　home a - wait - ing　　in the　　sky, Lord,＿ in the　　sky.

2. Lord, I told the undertaker,
   "Undertaker, please drive slow,
   For this body you are hauling,
   Lord, I hate to see her go."
   　　　　CHORUS

3. I followed close behind her,
   Tried to hold up and be brave,
   But I could not hide my sorrow
   When they laid her in the grave.
   　　　　CHORUS

4. Went back home, Lord. My home was lonesome
   Since my mother, she was gone.
   All my brothers, sisters, crying,
   What a home so sad and lone.
   　　　　CHORUS

YANKEE DOODLE

NEW ENGLAND

The melody of America's first national song can be traced to numerous European tunes. The lyrics are said to be by Richard Shuckburg, a British Army doctor intending to mock American troops in 1755. "Yankee" was the British word of contempt for New Englanders, "doodle" meant "fool," "dandy" meant one with affected manners and dress, and "macaroni" referred to decorations on uniforms. American troops enthusiastically adopted the song, and by 1781 were making the British dance to it. It has stayed a hit, fascinating modern composers such as Laurie Anderson, who calls it "the flip side to 'The Star-Spangled Banner.'"

Jaunty

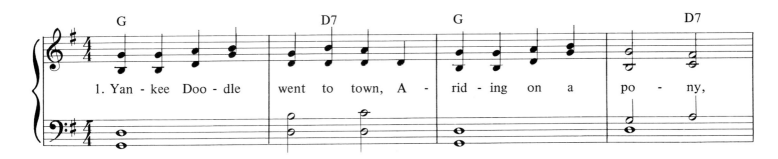

1. Yan - kee Doo - dle went to town, A - rid - ing on a po - ny,

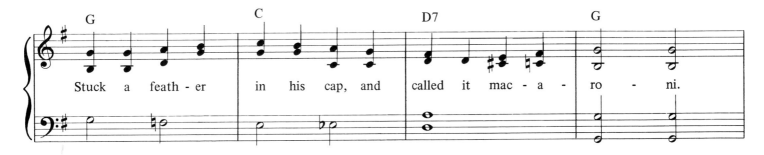

Stuck a feath - er in his cap, and called it mac - a - ro - ni.

CHORUS

Yan - kee Doo - dle, keep it up, Yan - kee Doo - dle dan - dy.

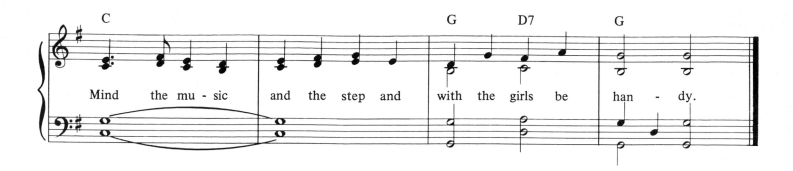

Mind the mu-sic and the step and with the girls be han-dy.

2. Father and I went down to camp along with Captain Gooding,
And there we saw both men and boys as thick as hasty pudding.
CHORUS

3. There was Captain Washington upon a slapping stallion,
Giving orders to his men—there must have been a million.
CHORUS

4. The troopers, they would gallop up and fire right in our faces;
It scared me almost half to death to see them run such races.
CHORUS

5. Then I saw a giant gun, large as a log of maple,
Upon a very little cart, a load for Father's cattle.
CHORUS

6. And every time they shot it off, it took a horn of powder
And made a noise like Father's gun, only a nation louder.
CHORUS

7. I can't tell you but half I saw, they kept up such a smother;
I took my hat off, made a bow, and scampered home to Mother.
CHORUS

8. "Yankee Doodle" is the tune Americans delight in;
'Twill do to whistle, sing, or play, and just the thing for fightin'.
CHORUS

Index of First Lines

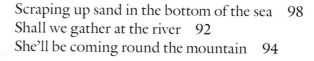

Index of Song Types

142

LOVE SONGS

LULLABIES

LUMBERJACK SONGS

NONSENSE OR BRAGGING SONGS

PATRIOTIC SONGS

PROTEST SONGS

TRAIN SONGS

WALTZES

WORK SONGS

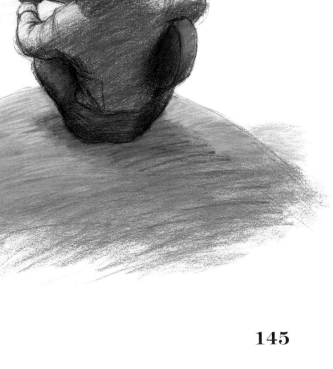

Kathleen Krull

is the author of several books for children and young adults, including *Songs of Praise,* an annotated collection of hymns, which *Booklist* called "a veritable feast for the ears, the eyes, and the heart." She studied music at Northwestern University, the North Shore Center of Music (Winnetka, Illinois), and Lawrence University, in Appleton, Wisconsin.

A lifelong folk music lover and a former children's book editor, Ms. Krull currently writes reviews for *The New York Times Book Review, The Los Angeles Times Book Review,* and *L.A. Parent* and *San Diego Parent* magazines. She lives with her husband in San Diego.

Allen Garns

is the versatile illustrator of book jackets, theater posters, and album covers. He has won awards from the Society of Illustrators, *Communication Arts,* and *American Illustration.* This is his first book for children.

Mr. Garns studied at the Art Center College of Design, in Pasadena, California. He lives with his wife and three children in Mesa, Arizona.

ABOUT THE *I HEAR AMERICA SINGING!* CD

When I was asked to record an album of traditional folk songs, I welcomed the opportunity. They are part of our musical heritage, and some are the very ones I learned to play when I first started strumming on my guitar at age eleven. I was pleased that the book includes all the verses and, except for two songs, so does the recording. I saw this project as a way to preserve for future generations the songs and their many verses, ones that often tell funny or sad stories about the making of America.

And on a more personal level, I knew this was an opportunity to work with old friends in a place far removed from New York City. Martha's Vineyard came to mind immediately, as it is the home of my old friend Mike Benjamin, a fine singer and guitarist, and also a place where mandolins and fishing rods outnumber taxi cabs.

After a late-night outdoor rehearsal, complete with vicious mosquitoes and home-brewed beer, we headed for Jim Parr's state-of-the-art recording facility in the basement of an old house in the town of Oak Bluffs. Two days later we had the recording completed, and I hope you enjoy listening to it as much as I enjoyed making it.

—Julian Harris
New York City

Julian Harris, a composer and musician, wrote more than 100 scores for the Disney/Henson TV show *Bear in the Big Blue House.*

VOCALISTS
Mike Benjamin: lead vocals, except where noted
Suzie Carmick: lead vocals on "Git Along, Little Dogies," "Red River Valley," and "Mama Don't Allow"
Derryll Brudzinski: lead vocals on "Buffalo Gals," "Down by the Riverside," and "The Sloop *John B.*"
Liam Bailey: lead vocals on "Home on the Range" and "Down in the Valley"
Julian Harris: lead vocals on "Clementine"
Jeanine Robbins: lead vocals on "Tell Me Why"
Judd Fuller: backing vocals

MUSICIANS
Mike Benjamin: lead guitar, acoustic guitar, and harmonica
Dick Neil: banjo, dobro, and mandolin
Liam Bailey: guitar, mandolin, and fiddle
Julian Harris: mandolin, guitar, and bass guitar
Judd Fuller: bass, lead guitar, and acoustic guitar
Robbie Soltz: drums and percussion
Paul Gordon: piano on "The Sloop *John B.*"
Jeremy Berlin: piano on "I've Been Working on the Railroad"
Aaron Wolfe: bass guitar on "The Erie Canal"

Arranged and produced by Julian Harris.
Additional production by Mike Benjamin.